Cyber Insurance Roundtable Readout Report

Grotius

Enhanced with Text Analytics by PageKicker
Robot Grotius

TL;DR: What could possibly go wrong?

PageKicker

fred@pagekicker.com

1521 Martha Avenue, Ann Arbor, Michigan, USA 48103

# About the Robot Author

## Grotius

Grotius

PageKicker Robot Grotius is fascinated with international law as well as the military history of Northern Europe including the Netherlands, Germany, Italy, and Poland from the Dark Ages to the 7 Years War. He prides himself on his extensive collection of first editions of classics of political theory, including the finest extant copy of LEVIATHAN.

Figure 1: Hugo Grotius

# Acknowledgements

I'd like to thank the enabling technologies that make me possible, including Bitnami, calibre, fbcmd, Magento, mySQL, nltk, pandoc, poppler, spyder, ttytter, and Ubuntu.

I'd also like to thank the people at PageKicker including Ken Leith, Brian Smiga, and Fred Zimmerman.

*Grotius*

# Programmatically Generated Summary

- The CISO reported that he meets with the Board of Trustees Audit Committee once a year to provide an overview of the HCO 1 cyber risk landscape; 5

  o o An Enterprise Risk Management Committee.

- The CISO advised that the Enterprise Risk Management Committee includes both an Executive Committee and Risk Management Process Owners; and o   The HCO 1 President's Cabinet and the HCO 1 Healthcare CEO.

- "In contrast, the initiatives you choose not to pursue (for good reason) will mean that there are known/anticipated risks that will not be addressed (at all in some cases) because the initiative is not undertaken." The CISO added that choosing not to fund these initiatives means that, intentionally or not, an organization also chooses to accept certain cyber risks as the cost of doing business.

- The CISO responded that the Department of Education asked specific, high-level questions of HCO 1 and that he and his team had provided background about the incident.

- The CISO advised that he's made the case to HCO 2 leadership that the same person should not be responsible for all network security needs.

- HIPAA'S LIMITS   The CISO reported that his fundamental concern with HIPAA as a cybersecurity "regulation" is that it doesn't effectively address his biggest security problem: the malicious hacking of EHRs and the medical IT infrastructure that supports their creation, sharing, and storage.

- The CISO replied that DAM can be useful for mitigating data breach risks but that even DAM processes many not provide sufficient clarity into the activities that are happening "at their source." He stated that thoroughly exploring all questionable 8 Data loss prevention (DLP) refers to systems that detect potential data breach and/or exfiltration transmissions and prevent them by monitoring, detecting, and blocking sensitive data while in-use (endpoint actions), in-motion (network traffic), and at-rest (data storage).

- "If we need to develop software and defeat hackers," he explained, "we do it and there's no need for the fanfare of a strategy to do it." He added that he nevertheless tries to link to "whatever strategy is in the works at the time" as a starting point before using tactics to actually fix the problems at hand.

- In the wake of the Sarbanes-Oxley Act, the company places an increasingly high priority on enhancing its reporting processes.17 The RMD explained that for all four of these overarching risk categories, each HCO 3 operating company tailors its related policies, processes, and programs to address the specific circumstances and unique requirements of its host jurisdiction.

- He advised that HCO 3 has a well-established cyber risk management cycle that includes a lengthy list of cyber incidents that might impact the company and corresponding mitigations and controls that are specifically "road-mapped" to address them.

- The GOCD replied that HCO 3 does not currently carry cybersecurity insurance, relying instead on its aforementioned cyber risk management cycle and cyber incident run book to direct actions based on perceived costs and benefits to the company.

- He added that while HCO 3 is concerned about cyber risks that pose financial and/or reputational harm, both the cyber risk management cycle and cyber incident run book focus on cyber risks that could cause significant operational disruption.

- "The operational impact of an anticipated cyber incident determines its priority," he explained, "and directly informs the communication of an actual incident to the board." An IT professional then asked, given HCO 3's decision not to purchase cybersecurity insurance, whether or not HCO 3 self-insures or alternatively assumes the cost of a cyber incident when it occurs.

# Readability Report

Flesh-Kincaid Grade Level: 14.79

Flesh Reading Ease Score: 28.56

Sentences: 799

Words: 17,729

Average Syllables per Word: 1.84

Average Words per Sentence: 22.19

# Explanation

The Flesch/Flesch–Kincaid readability tests are designed to indicate comprehension difficulty when reading a passage of contemporary academic English. There are two tests: the Flesch Reading Ease and the Flesch–Kincaid Grade Level. Although they use the same core measures (word length and sentence length), they have different weighting factors. The results of the two tests correlate approximately inversely: a text with a comparatively high score on the Reading Ease test should have a lower score on the Grade Level test. Rudolf Flesch devised both systems while J. Peter Kincaid developed the latter for the United States Navy.

The Flesch-Kincaid grade level corresponds to a US education grade level, where higher grades are expected to understand more challenging material.

In the Flesch Reading Ease test, higher scores indicate material that is easier to read. Typical scores: Reader's Digest 65, Time Magazine 52, Harvard Law Review 30.

There is a good discussion at

http://en.wikipedia.org/wiki/Flesch%E2%80%93Kincaid_readability_test.

# Unique Proper Nouns and Key Terms

administrator

analyst

Arlington

Asset Management and Software Security Solutions

back office

Brazil

BRIC

business process

car manufacturers

CEO

chief financial officer

Chief Information Security Officer

chief risk officer

Chief Risk Officer

Chief Technology Officer

China

CIO

CISO

consumerproducts

consumer products

Coordination Center

cost/benefit analysis

CTO

Cyber Insurance

Cybersecurity Insurance

CYBERSECURITY INSURANCE

Cybersecurity Insurance Roundtable

cyber threat

DAM

data integrity

data storage

deep packet inspection

DHS

DoD

E-Government Act of 2002

encryption software

end user

Enterprise Risk Management Committee

ERM

ERM Council

ERP

EU

EU Safe Harbor

Executive

EXECUTIVE

Executive Committee

Executive Committee and Risk Management

Federal Government

federal law

federal law enforcement

fraud

GOCD

Grey Market

handheld devices

HCO

Health Care Organization

Healthcare Privacy Officer

healthcare system

Health Information Technology

Health Information Technology for Economic and Clinical

# Cyber Insurance Roundtable Readout Report

## Health Care and Cyber Risk Management: Cost/Benefit Approaches

National Protection and Programs Directorate
Department of Homeland Security

*February 2014*

# TABLE OF CONTENTS

## BACKGROUND

The Department of Homeland Security's (DHS) National Protection and Programs Directorate (NPPD) helps both private and public sector partners secure their cyber networks, assisting them collectively and individually and improving the nation's overall cybersecurity posture in the process. Through these interactions, DHS has become aware of a growing interest in cybersecurity insurance as well as limitations in the current market – especially when it comes to first-party market coverage for cyber-related critical infrastructure loss.[1] To better understand those limitations and how a more robust market could help encourage better cyber risk management, NPPD hosted its first-ever Cybersecurity Insurance Workshop during the fall of 2012. NPPD had two main goals for the event: (1) determine what obstacles prevent carriers from offering more attractive first-party policies to more customers at lower cost; and (2) promote stakeholder discussion about how to move the market forward.

At that event, NPPD hosted a diverse group of participants, registered on a first-come, first-served basis, from five stakeholder groups that included insurance carriers, risk managers, information technology/cyber experts, academics/social scientists, and critical infrastructure owners and operators. Several federal agencies also sent representatives. As part of its planning, NPPD asked participants to nominate breakout group topics in order to develop the workshop agenda and ensure that it addressed matters of critical interest. Participants nominated the following topics, which focused specifically on the first-party market: (1) Defining Insurable and Uninsurable Cyber Risks; (2) Cyber Insurance and the Human Element; (3) Cyber Liability: Who is Responsible for What Harm; (4) Current Cyber Risk Management Strategies and Approaches; (5) Cyber Insurance: What Harms Should It Cover and What Should It Cost; (6) Improving the Cyber Insurance Market: Stakeholder Roles and Responsibilities; and (7) Sequencing Solutions: How Should the Market Move Forward?

On May 13, 2013, NPPD held a roundtable based on what it had learned during the fall workshop. The roundtable focused on how organizations should go about building more effective cyber risk cultures as a prerequisite to a stronger and more responsive first-party market. With representatives from each of the same stakeholder groups in attendance, NPPD led a discussion about four "pillars" of such cultures: (1) Engaged Executive Leadership; (2) Targeted Cyber Risk Management and Awareness; (3) Cost-Effective Technology Investments Tailored to Organizational Needs; and (4) Relevant Information Sharing. Participants described the importance of and challenges with implementing the pillars in three distinct but related contexts: within companies; between partnering companies; and nationally. They likewise offered their opinions about how large, mid-size, and small companies should go about meeting those challenges given their traditionally disparate levels of expertise and risk management resources.

---

[1] First-party cybersecurity insurance policies cover direct losses to companies arising from events such as business interruption, destruction of data and property, and reputational harm. Third party policies, by contrast, cover losses that a company causes to its customers and others, such as harms arising from the exposure of personally identifiable information (PII) through a data breach. *See* U.S. Department of Homeland Security. *Cybersecurity Insurance Workshop Readout Report*. ONLINE. 2012. National Protection and Programs Directorate. Available: http://www.dhs.gov/publication/cybersecurity-insurance [29 January 2014].

During both events, participants shared a wide range of perspectives on these various topics, which were included in workshop and roundtable readout reports. The reports are available on the DHS Cybersecurity Insurance webpage at http://www.dhs.gov/publication/cybersecurity-insurance.

Building on the ideas surfaced at the workshop and roundtable, and after conducting its own additional research, NPPD publicly announced its intent to convene a second roundtable in the fall of 2013. That event, the subject of this readout report, addressed a fundamental yet unanswered question that had arisen over the course of the prior discussions: how do cost and benefit considerations inform the identification of not only an organization's top cyber risks but also appropriate risk management investments to address them? On November 20, 2013, NPPD accordingly hosted a small number of participants, registered on a first-come, first-served basis, at the National Intellectual Property Rights (IPR) Coordination Center in Arlington, Virginia, to find answers.

NPPD adopted a new format for the roundtable that included three cyber risk management use case presentations by health care organization (HCO) representatives. The representatives described an actual cyber incident that their organizations had experienced; how they managed the incident; and how lessons learned from the incident have influenced their actions and investments to improve patient safety. The presentations likewise addressed how the organizations are incorporating cost/benefit considerations as part of cyber risk management strategies; how their individual risk cultures are evolving as a result; and what role cybersecurity insurance is playing as part of their processes. An extended group discussion period followed each use case presentation in order to examine all of these themes in detail and to identify potential opportunities to enhance cyber risk management best practices.

Prior to the roundtable, NPPD advised the presenters and participants alike that their input during the event would be included in this final readout report on a non-attribution basis. NPPD explained that the purpose of this report would be to: (1) capture diverse ideas about how cost/benefit considerations motivate cyber risk management investments, including insurance investments; and (2) record a wide range of perspectives that might inform cyber risk management efforts nationally. NPPD further advised that it wasn't looking for, wouldn't accept, and wouldn't solicit group or consensus recommendations during the roundtable. NPPD likewise clarified that neither DHS nor NPPD would make any decisions about agency policy or positions during the event. In addition to 8 roundtable leaders, organizers, and support personnel, NPPD hosted 30 participants from the following stakeholder groups:

- Insurance Carriers:                                    7
- Risk Managers:                                         6
- Information Technology/Cyber Experts:                  6
- Academics/Social Scientists:                           3
- Critical Infrastructure Owners/Operators:             5
- Government:                                            3

## EXECUTIVE SUMMARY

The HCO representatives, all of them Chief Information Security Officers (CISOs) or risk manager equivalents, hailed from a variety of organizations including an academic medical center and research university, a university hospital system, and a medical vendor that provides health care consumer products, pharmaceuticals, and medical devices/technology. Although each presented very different cyber risk management use cases, they shared many of the same challenges while addressing them. They consequently directed their remarks to three principal topics during the roundtable discussions: (1) making the case for cybersecurity investments to senior leadership; (2) incorporating cost/benefit considerations into their arguments; and (3) negotiating the boundary between risk mitigation efforts and risk transfer/insurance options to promote more effective cyber risk management strategies.

### ENGAGING LEADERSHIP

The HCO representatives described two approaches to driving cybersecurity investments within their respective organizations. Several emphasized the value of enterprise risk management (ERM) to their efforts, noting that involving senior leadership in both the identification and prioritization of cyber risks has been critical to building trust in and promoting the effectiveness of their teams. They explained how they create master lists of priority cyber risks and corresponding risk controls for leadership review, drawing heavily on their team members' subject matter expertise as informed by real world cyber incidents. After presenting and discussing his team's list, one representative reported that his board of directors literally "draws a line" between those controls that will be funded given available resources and those controls that will not. This practice, he noted, generates a sense of ownership by the board that invests it in the success of its chosen approaches. By contrast, another representative explained that more primal factors motivate his leadership to spend against cyber risk: namely, fear of substantial regulatory fines and "public shaming" under the Health Insurance Portability and Accountability Act (HIPAA).[2] The representative advised that even though HIPAA does not focus on malicious hacking or other activity that doesn't directly impact the delivery of patient care, he nevertheless tries to market all his recommended risk controls on HIPAA grounds. Given its role as "primary driver of IT security funding," he observed, HIPAA currently serves as a necessary – albeit imperfect – vehicle for obtaining the cybersecurity funds he needs. Despite these disparate approaches, the HCO representatives concurred that ERM strategies that include cyber risk become easier to develop, fund, and implement once senior leaders mature their understanding of the full range of online dangers their organizations face.

### COSTS AND BENEFITS

The HCO representatives likewise advised that when it comes to cost/benefit considerations, they use an exclusively qualitative approach when prioritizing cyber risks on the one hand and making the case for cyber risk management resources on the other. They asserted that cyber risk management today – at least in the health care sector – is more of an art than a science. One representative explained that his senior leadership usually defers to him regarding "top cyber risks" so long as he

---

[2] The Health Insurance Portability and Accountability Act of 1996 (Pub.L. 104-191; 110 Stat. 1936).

maintains a keen sense of what's happening on his organization's networks, what's likely to happen on them in the future, and where the greatest potential for financial and other loss exists. This trust in his expertise likewise carries over directly to his proposed solution sets. Spreadsheets with quantitative details about the merits of one risk control over another, he continued, consequently have little to do with convincing corporate leaders to act. Several representatives agreed and reported that their leadership instead encourages them to "ballpark" their cybersecurity investment recommendations "in relation to the pack." As one noted, the rule of thumb is to spend not so much more than their peers that shareholders get angry and not so much less that regulators come knocking.

The representatives agreed that getting their organizations to actually *fund* their cybersecurity investment recommendations is the hard part. One stated that the best way for him to "sell" a particular investment's benefit is to assign ownership for potential cyber incident losses to specific individuals. He explained that once department heads understand that they're institutionally on the hook for such losses, resource conversations about purchasing and pre-positioning various risk controls suddenly become much easier. Another advised that avoiding the costs of a HIPAA audit typically is the only "benefit" he needs to demonstrate regarding a proposed mitigation. In short, casting a cyber risk control's benefits in terms of avoiding direct financial pain appears to be a highly successful technique.

## THE ROLE OF INSURANCE

The HCO representatives were somewhat ambivalent about the role of cybersecurity insurance within their organizations' cyber risk management strategies. Several reported that they meet annually with underwriters to provide updates about their organization's cyber incidents and believe that data breach coverage in particular is "good to have." While one appreciated that his employer's insurer paid for an incident response firm to help out during a major cyber incident, he stated that he saw cybersecurity insurance as a way to address "catastrophic" situations only. He emphasized that he would *not* welcome insurers dictating how he or his team should mitigate cyber risks in his day-to-day environment. While another representative concurred that cybersecurity insurance has value because it purports to cover costs arising from unavoidable data breaches, he was dubious about the level of reimbursement his organization could truly expect in the event of a breach. It's never made a claim to test its policy. The third representative advised, in turn, that his organization has not yet invested in cybersecurity insurance. In view of his limited cybersecurity resources, he added, it makes more sense to spend on risk mitigation rather than risk transfer options.

Under these circumstances, the roundtable participants agreed that both cybersecurity professionals and insurers would benefit from a sustained dialogue about what each community brings to the cyber risk management table. Several remarked that a good first topic of conversation would be how they could work together to advance the cybersecurity insurance market's ability to cover cyber-related critical infrastructure loss.

## HEALTH CARE ORGANIZATION 1

ORGANIZATION OVERVIEW: The Chief Information Security Officer (CISO) for Health Care Organization 1 (HCO 1) described HCO 1 as a nationally top-ranked research university and academic medical center. HCO 1 comprises several hospitals and hosts influential and sometimes controversial faculty and alumni – the profiles of whom, he noted, sometimes make it a cyber target. He stated that HCO 1 is home to almost 15,000 students; 28,000 faculty and staff; and 500 central information technology (IT) staff. The CISO advised that HCO 1 employs eight full-time information security staff. Four of those professionals work on operational and tactical information security issues such as establishing firewalls and providing hardware and software tokens. The remaining four focus on more strategic issues. Two of those four, he added, work strictly on IT compliance matters. The CISO described his team's budget as "small." Apart from employee salaries, he receives less than a million dollars annually to fund cyber risk management initiatives.

USE CASE PRESENTATION AND DISCUSSION:

CYBER RISK LANDSCAPE

- The CISO described HCO 1 as having a "high" threat environment in which his team, on a monthly basis, quarantines and/or blocks approximately 450 new bad actors; 30 million communications attempts to and from bad actors; seven million malicious websites; and 60 million emails. By contrast, his team supports the secure delivery of approximately six million emails. The CISO added that threat actors that target HCO 1 typically include identity thieves, phishers and spammers, and nation states.

- The CISO next described the number of cyber incidents that he and his team must respond to on an annual basis. They include anywhere from 400 to 500 minor incidents, including unauthorized beaconing out of the HCO 1 network (indicating malware or spyware); 10 to 15 "significant" incidents such as identity theft schemes that directly engage his team; and one to five breach notifications. One to three of those breach notifications, he added, include reportable events under HIPAA. The CISO advised that his team routinely cooperates with local and federal law enforcement on such incidents.

HCO 1 RISK MANAGEMENT CULTURE

GOVERNANCE

- The CISO stated that he believes that HCO 1 has a "healthy risk culture" when it comes to managing its cyber risk environment. He explained that HCO 1 has six governance bodies that support his team's cybersecurity work. They include:

  - A Board of Trustees Audit Committee. The CISO reported that he meets with the Board of Trustees Audit Committee once a year to provide an overview of the HCO 1 cyber risk landscape;

- o The HCO 1 President's Cabinet and the HCO 1 Healthcare CEO. The CISO stated that he meets with these individuals multiple times per year, as necessary;

- o An Enterprise Risk Management Committee. The CISO advised that the Enterprise Risk Management Committee includes both an Executive Committee and Risk Management Process Owners; and

- o A Breach Notification Team. The CISO explained that the Breach Notification Team includes the HCO 1 Chief Information Officer (CIO), the CISO (himself), the General Counsel, and the Chief Risk Officer – all of whom have responsibility for both the HCO 1 healthcare system and the university – as well as the University Privacy Officer, the Healthcare Privacy Officer, the HIPAA Steering Committee (which monitors HCO 1's HIPAA compliance), and an IT Steering Committee (which centralizes IT efforts across HCO 1).

- • The CISO advised that these governance bodies are comfortable making hard cyber risk management decisions and accordingly will take inconvenient mitigation steps; notify parties affected by a cyber incident; and accept institutional risk, when appropriate. He explained that HCO 1 leadership is guided by a desire to make the "right" cyber risk management decisions for impacted individuals within the HCO 1 community and for HCO 1 as an institution, in that order.

  - o The CISO reported that the governance bodies involved in HCO 1 cyber incident response include the Breach Notification Team, the Enterprise Risk Management Executive Committee, and business unit leaders from business units impacted by cyber incidents.

  - o The CISO noted that the Enterprise Risk Management Committee worked collaboratively to reduce an original list of 1,600 priority risks to 60 risks – three of which involve data breach and/or exposure risks. He advised that his team meets with the Committee several times a year to provide updates on the state of HCO 1's cybersecurity risk. He explained that his primary responsibility, as the cyber risk management process owner, is to get the right information to the Committee in order to enable effective management of the most pressing cyber risks.

  - o The CISO further explained that after a cyber incident, the Breach Notification Team gathers the relevant facts and generates a one-to-two page, high-level risk document with recommendations on how it thinks HCO 1 should respond to the incident. The Team then provides its recommendations to the Enterprise Risk Management Committee which, in turn, determines what actions to take.

- An IT professional asked about the mechanics of the Breach Notification Team process. The CISO replied that it usually takes a short but significant amount of time to conduct a fact-finding effort in support of the one-to-two page Breach Notification Team report. He added that the process – from initial notification of a breach to final decision by the Enterprise Risk Management Committee – can address both cyber and physical threats. For example, HCO 1 maintains its own police department to which the Breach Notification Team can provide "trackable" leads such as phone calls. The CISO stated that the police department in turn can issue subpoenas, an authority which it has exercised on his team's behalf in the past. In return, he noted, his team can provide technical expertise for law enforcement tasks such as forensic analysis of infected workstations.

- A risk manager asked the CISO about his communications strategy following a cyber incident. He responded that his team puts together the first draft of any message in order to ensure that all the technical and other facts about an event are correct. The team then sends the draft to the HCO 1 press office for final preparation. The CISO added that he and his staff are very cognizant of all the downstream impacts that might result from an incident and that that knowledge informs everything they do. An IT professional then asked whether the CISO has a "holding" press statement "at the ready" whenever cyber incidents occur. The CISO responded in the negative.

- A critical infrastructure representative asked what participation the CISO has in "higher-level discussions for business decisions." The CISO responded that although neither he nor his team directly participate in discussions about large and strategic IT purchases, the Chief Information Officer (CIO) does so participate and is "very security minded." The CISO added that if HCO 1 considered such a purchase, the CIO would come to him and ask for advice and guidance.

## *STRATEGIES FOR SUCCESS*

- The CISO described a two-pronged strategy for his team's cyber risk management success that includes obtaining leadership approval for HCO 1's Strategic Plan for Information Security and involving leadership in the incident response process itself.

## *STRATEGIC PLAN*

- Regarding the first prong, the CISO advised that his team works to align HCO 1's Strategic Plan for Information Security, which addresses where large information security initiatives should be focused for HCO 1 in the coming 18-36 months, with HCO 1's overall institutional vision and strategy. As part of that effort, his team generates a prioritized list of information security risks every 12-18 months. That list includes a corresponding series of information security initiatives designed to address those prioritized risks. Each such initiative includes a description of its estimated one-time and recurring costs; staffing requirements; and the specific risks – e.g., those arising out of Bring Your Own Device (BYOD) and other business trends – that they're designed to address.[3] The CISO advised that he seeks funding for the highest priority initiatives recommended by his team but has HCO 1 leadership literally "draw a line" between the information security initiatives that it will fund and those which it will not.

- The CISO reported that this decision process highlights to HCO 1 leadership that, in a resource-constrained environment, some threats will not be addressed. In this way, leadership is forced to explicitly prioritize between different types of threats and risks and accordingly "own" its final decisions in a much more complete manner. He stated that HCO 1 executives have accordingly become more and more invested over time in the success of the HCO 1 Strategic Plan for Information Security.

- A critical infrastructure representative asked if the CISO sometimes argues in the "opposite" direction, attempting to convince his leadership not to fund specific initiatives that may not offer a comparative value. He responded that his team does not make such arguments but that the CIO is much more likely to do so.

*LEADERSHIP INVOLVEMENT IN INCIDENT RESPONSE*

- Regarding the second prong, the CISO reported that his team provides regular cybersecurity briefings to HCO 1's six governance bodies – a service that has gone a long way toward building a "great relationship" with key leaders and establishing his team's credibility. As a result, he has obtained leadership approval for not only a unified cyber incident/breach response process but also incident/breach response teams to actually implement that process. To fortify this progress, the CISO ensures that HCO 1 leadership has final decision making responsibility for all strategic cyber risk management decisions that impact the incident/breach response process.

- The CISO emphasized that his team's efforts have resulted in strong leadership support for a predetermined funding model that imposes the direct costs of cyber incidents on the HCO 1 business units responsible for them. The CISO mentioned that he wants those units to "share the pain" that their sometimes poor cybersecurity causes to the enterprise. Using an internal billing code, he accordingly charges them for breach notification, investigation, and mitigation expenses as they arise and accrue over time. The CISO noted that this cost ownership policy is meant to reduce reliance on institutional risk across HCO 1. He stated that this approach is very effective and that he rarely, if ever, feels that he's being asked to internalize too much risk.

---

[3] Bring Your Own Device (BYOD) refers to the practice of allowing an organization's employees to use their own computers, smartphones, or other devices for work purposes. Oxford Dictionaries. BYOD. ONLINE. N.D. Available: http://www.oxforddictionaries.com/us/definition/american_english/ [7 January 2014].

- In the summer of 2013, HCO 1's network monitoring tools alerted security administrators that an unexpected system management tool had executed on several systems. The security team investigated the activity and determined that administrative accounts were accessing systems in a manner that suggested that they had been compromised by malicious hackers. HCO 1's initial investigative efforts revealed that at least a partial list of domain accounts and password hashes had been compromised by the malicious hackers and that they had obtained the credentials of at least two domain administrators.

- To assist with forensic analysis and other security efforts involved with the incident, HCO 1 engaged the assistance of one of the nation's leading incident response firms. Doing so took several days because HCO 1 first had to verify that its insurer would pay for the services – the costs for which exceeded insurance policy limits – before entering into negotiations with the firm. HCO 1 actively cooperated with federal law enforcement agents during this time. Through its combined investigative efforts, HCO 1 was able to determine that approximately 44 systems within the HCO 1 environment were either compromised or accessed by the malicious hackers. Other than the aforementioned list of user accounts and hashed passwords, the investigation did not find evidence that the malicious hackers had accessed additional personally identifiable information (PII).

- HCO 1 took immediate steps to investigate and contain the intrusion, including the disabling of privileged accounts to which the malicious hackers had access and replacing potentially compromised Active Directory servers. In conjunction with HCO 1's Enterprise Security team, the incident response firm performed investigative activities both onsite and remotely for just over five weeks.

- The incident response firm asked HCO 1 not to remove the malicious hackers immediately in order to provide it with sufficient time to figure out what they were up to on the HCO 1 network. The CISO and his team accordingly recommended to HCO 1's Enterprise Risk Management Committee that they initially make a very limited mitigation response so the firm could conduct its requested assessment. The Enterprise Risk Management Committee agreed. After determining the full scope of systems impacted by the incident, a second round of remediation activities were identified and planned. In addition to finally removing the malicious hackers from the environment, those planned activities were designed to improve HCO 1's defenses and enhance its monitoring capabilities over the long-term.

- HCO 1 initiated the second round of remediation activities two weeks after the incident response firm began its onsite activities. At that time, HCO 1 launched an enterprise-wide password change;[4] removed any remaining compromised systems that had been identified through the ongoing investigation; blocked communication with known malicious hacker network addresses and domains; and implemented hardening countermeasures to make it more difficult for malicious hackers to regain access to HCO 1's internal network and to move about within it. Additionally, HCO 1 implemented enhanced monitoring and alerting capabilities to help detect future attacks.

- HCO 1 currently is working on several additional long-term efforts to improve its ability to prevent, detect, and respond to similar events in the future.

*LESSONS LEARNED AND RULES OF THUMB*

- The CISO and his team identified seven "lessons learned and rules of thumb" following the use case incident that continue to inform their strategic cyber risk management planning across the HCO 1 enterprise:

  o *Carpe Incident! Be prepared to take advantage of funding opportunities that may arise from a cyber incident.*

    The CISO stated that very often during or immediately after a significant cyber incident, leadership will ask questions like, "Is there anything we can do to keep this kind of thing from happening again?" "Do you need any additional resources to help resolve this?" "Is there any assistance we can provide?" He advised that if cybersecurity professionals have security initiatives "waiting in the wings" solely because of funding or staffing limitations, they should seize this moment to ask for the additional resources they need. In short, having a small portfolio of pre-prepared, ready-to-go project proposals might just be the thing that will turn a bad situation into an opportunity for improvement.

  o *During extended incident response efforts, having all the members of an incident response team share the same physical space while doing their work is extremely beneficial.*

    The CISO explained that he co-located malware analysts and network engineers throughout the duration of the incident response cycle, an arrangement that led to many efficiencies and synergies in terms of communications, coordination, and situational awareness. These efficiencies and synergies were important, he observed, because approximately 500 individuals across HCO 1 and associated organizations, including the incident response firm, were involved in the response effort.

---

[4] The CISO stated that many individuals within the HCO 1 community were likely using their HCO 1 passwords for their personal accounts. HCO 1 didn't want anyone's personal accounts to be affected by the incident, so it chose to notify everyone of the need to change the passwords for those accounts.

The CISO added that he'd tell insurance companies that paying for an outside incident response firm to conduct an on-site, real-time assessment of a cyber incident is money well spent. He advised that the costs involved with the use case firm totaled $300,000. By comparison, he commented, traditional off-site forensic analysis "would have cost an order of magnitude more and would have been slower."

- <u>Things are seldom as definitive as they may seem during the early stages of an incident, so CISOs should not overstate or understate the "facts."</u>

  The CISO suggested that cybersecurity professionals should manage the expectations of their organization's leadership by phrasing their messaging carefully – saying, for example, "the incident is fluid, and this is what we believe at this time" – and then providing more detailed and precise updates as more (and better) information becomes available.

- <u>A decision not to fund a security initiative is a de facto risk acceptance decision and needs to be made by someone with the authority to accept such risks.</u>

  The CISO noted that most security incidents don't result from completely novel attack vectors. On the contrary, he continued, most of the potential avenues of compromise likely have been anticipated and potential solutions identified in advance. The CISO added that the real issue is that cybersecurity professionals typically can't do everything at once, so tradeoffs must be made based on priority. "When you're choosing which initiatives to implement you should be doing so because those solutions are believed to provide the highest value in terms of risk reduction versus cost/impact to your organization," he stated. "In contrast, the initiatives you choose not to pursue (for good reason) will mean that there are known/anticipated risks that will not be addressed (at all in some cases) because the initiative is not undertaken."

  The CISO added that choosing not to fund these initiatives means that, intentionally or not, an organization also chooses to accept certain cyber risks as the cost of doing business. He added that such a decision may be entirely rational, but that the people making it should have not only sufficient budgetary authority to do so but also sufficient management authority to accept the level of anticipated risk that will result. These are joint decisions, he emphasized, that should be decided together by the same people at an enterprise-wide level.

- <u>A system compromise is not the same thing as a data breach.</u>

  Knowing early that malicious hacker(s) have not accessed data, the CISO explained, can save incident responders a lot of time, effort, and expense.

o   Proactively instrumenting an IT environment is critical to effectively managing a cyber
    incident.

    The CISO explained that he and his team had pre-positioned most of its instrumentation
    prior to the use case incident but only because they hadn't had it in place before other
    previous incidents. Even so, he continued, HCO 1 had not pre-positioned the solutions
    that the incident response firm ultimately provided – solutions that made a huge impact
    during and after the use case incident. As a result, HCO 1 is now deploying those
    solutions on a permanent basis to assist with future incidents.

o   Vulnerabilities in "non-critical" systems can lead to the compromise of critical systems.

    The CISO advised that HCO 1 had multi-factor authentication in place for its critical
    systems prior to the use case incident. He noted that the vulnerability that the
    malicious hacker(s) exploited, however, existed on a non-critical system that did not
    require two-factor identification. Once the malicious hacker(s) gained access to that
    system, he added, they worked laterally across the entire HCO 1 network.

### COST/BENEFIT CONSIDERATIONS

- The CISO explained that HCO 1's approach to identifying top cyber risks and appropriate
  controls to address them is qualitative and not quantitative. He explained that a qualitative
  approach focuses his team on the relative priority and ordinal ranking of cybersecurity
  initiatives – as outlined in the HCO 1 Strategic Plan for Information Security – that in turn inform
  which specific cyber risk management investments to make. To generate that ranking, the CISO
  added, his team relies heavily on its own cybersecurity knowledge and expertise. "Cybersecurity
  is an art," he observed, "not a science." When asked whether he felt pressure to justify his
  recommendations using return on investment (ROI) analyses, the CISO responded, "It would
  dilute our message to just put numbers on a spreadsheet. Our relationship with management is
  based on trust."

- The CISO explained that when it comes to cost/benefit considerations, information security
  "generally carries a big stick" across the HCO 1 environment. That big stick, he continued,
  derives in part from the organization's ongoing defense of a class action lawsuit involving the
  lost PII of several thousand people. The CISO noted that the lawsuit powerfully drives home to
  HCO 1 leadership every day the cost/benefit reality of information security investment.

- The CISO advised that he and his team do not prioritize their risk mitigation efforts in isolation
  but in direct reference to the leadership-approved HCO 1 Strategic Plan for Information Security.
  "Everything sounds like a good idea in a vacuum," he observed, and therefore must be
  considered in relation to the strategic plan. Doing so, he continued, helps ensure that the team
  does not overreact to the "threat of the week." The CISO added, "We do not want to try to do
  everything and fail in everything due to lack of resources."

- The CISO noted, however, that he and team sometimes "rank order" their strategic mitigation efforts alongside non-mitigation initiatives of potential benefit to the organization. For example, they might treat inexpensive "quick wins" as operational initiatives worthy of action and will fund them accordingly.

- Finally, the CISO advised that his team has been able to reduce costs by leveraging pre-negotiated contracts such as the one with the incident response firm retained during the use case incident last summer. When asked by an insurer whether HCO 1 sustained additional costs beyond retention costs for that firm, the CISO reported that the enterprise had also suffered a "loss in productivity."

*USE CASE QUESTIONS*

- A critical infrastructure representative asked if HCO 1 had taken forensic images of the described attacks; whether it had been able to determine the identity of the malicious hacker(s); and the extent to which law enforcement provided value. The CISO responded that most of HCO 1's systems were running on virtual machines, so his team easily created necessary forensic images, captured memory, and produced disk images. He added that HCO 1 had "flow data for days" on its network as well as network packet capture solutions that retain 28-30 hours of network traffic into and out of the organization at a time. "Every time we identified a suspect system," the CISO added, "we added it to our list [for network packet capture]." He advised, however, that neither the incident response firm nor law enforcement had been able to confirm the identity of the malicious hacker(s). While work continues in this area, he explained, the malicious hacker(s) did not appear to match other known actors. The CISO observed, moreover, that information sharing with federal law enforcement during the incident had proven to be a largely one-way affair, although his federal partners during their investigation had been able to identify four or five additional "bad guy" systems that had been communicating with HCO 1 servers.

- A risk manager asked whether the CISO believed that HCO 1 has a trusted network with other universities. The CISO responded affirmatively and advised that HCO 1 is involved with the Research and Education Networking Information Sharing Analysis Center (REN-ISAC). He added that during the use case incident, HCO 1 reached out to similarly-situated health care organizations through the REN-ISAC who were also experiencing attacks. The CISO asserted that the nation needs an "ISAC of ISACs" so organizations from multiple sectors can share cyber risk and cyber incident information in real time.

- An insurer asked what kinds of interactions HCO 1 had or is having with regulators in the wake of the use case incident. The CISO responded that the Department of Education asked specific, high-level questions of HCO 1 and that he and his team had provided background about the incident. He advised that although user IDs and passwords appeared to have been exposed during the event, there have been no indications that other PII was compromised.

- An IT professional asked how long it took to get the incident response firm on site. The CISO responded that a contract was signed within several days; gear was shipped and installed a few days after that; and that the firm – once it arrived – took 17 days to "figure out what was going on." The CISO and his team were very pleased with the firm's performance and, as previously noted, plan to maintain their business relationship.

- A second IT professional asked if HCO 1 was happy with its insurer's support during the incident. The CISO responded affirmatively, noting that HCO 1 had paid the required deductible and that the carrier covered all the costs beyond that amount. He added that the carrier had helped HCO 1 get better prices for services in some cases – typically from approved vendors – and that requiring the use of approved vendors was a reasonable demand from his perspective.

## CYBERSECURITY INSURANCE

- The CISO advised that HCO 1 has maintained cybersecurity insurance since 2008 and that he considers it to be the cyber equivalent to a catastrophic health plan – in short, it provides limited coverage with a large deductible. In response to a question from a risk manager, he advised that he's fairly isolated from the financial side of insurance and that his only interaction with the insurer in that respect is to "answer their annual [information security] questionnaire." While the CISO stated that HCO 1's risk transfer needs are being met by its existing policies – especially when it came to getting the incident response firm on-site quickly – he identified several gaps that he'd like to see the broader cybersecurity insurance market fill:

  o Identity theft insurance for breach notification recipients, so individuals who experience fraud and related losses as a result of a breach can be made whole;

  o Elimination of exceptions for widespread incidents such as Internet worms and viruses; and

  o Coverage that applies to HCO 1 data regardless of where it "lives" – for example, beyond HCO 1's network to BYOD devices and Cloud/SaaS Services.

- The CISO added that he would not welcome additional cybersecurity "regulations" being imposed by HCO 1's insurer through the insurance contract.

## HEALTH CARE ORGANIZATION 2

ORGANIZATION OVERVIEW: The Chief Information Security Officer (CISO) for Health Care Organization 2 (HCO 2) described HCO 2 as an enterprise that includes six major hospitals, over 100 clinics, and a university system that includes a medical community of almost 60,000 members. It serves millions of patients. Given HCO 2's size, he explained, he doesn't have to look hard for examples of cyber incidents that occur within it. The CISO stated that HCO 2's network security team employs approximately 30 full time equivalent (FTE) employees. He advised that approximately 15 of those FTEs are application security specialists, meaning that they set up rules dictating user access to systems. He added that approximately seven other FTEs work directly on network security issues while another seven focus on acquisitions or "buying security."

The CISO commented that his team currently lacks risk management experts and "data cops." Finding and hiring specialists in these areas is difficult, he explained, because they have inherently tough and thankless jobs. The CISO advised that he's made the case to HCO 2 leadership that the same person should not be responsible for all network security needs. He commented that the cybersecurity field is very specialized and that the person handling laptop encryption, for example, should not also be working on network security. As the cyber threat continues to escalate, he added, the need for specialized cybersecurity professionals will increase accordingly.

USE CASE PRESENTATION AND DISCUSSION:

*CYBER RISK LANDSCAPE*

- The CISO described the HCO 2 cyber risk landscape, and the cyber risk landscape for health care organizations generally, through the prism of electronic health records (EHRs) and the increasing number of security issues involving them.

*LONGSTANDING CHALLENGES*

- The CISO observed that most doctors still use paper medical records despite the fact that health care providers have been talking about implementing EHRs since the 1960s. He noted that the transition to EHRs has been slow for two main reasons.

  o First, system designers often don't put the needs of end users – i.e., the doctors – first. Instead, they develop underlying infrastructure to support the creation, transfer, and storage of EHRs before they build out end user applications. The CISO commented that strict usability requirements of the medical profession create a high performance bar for the technology that must be satisfied before doctors will adopt it. For example, he explained, doctors examining patients can't wait minutes at a time for EHRs to load onto handheld devices. In addition to cutting into the doctor's efficiency – and, consequently, his or her profit margin – inadequate technology (i.e., the end user application) and/or the perception thereof erodes patient confidence.

o <u>Second</u>, EHR statutory and/or regulatory requirements themselves impose significant technical challenges that must be successfully addressed. The CISO described the two primary components of medical record exchange in most practices:

   ➢ Documentation, the so-called "easy" part, such as when a doctor prescribes a medicine for a patient; and

   ➢ Order entry, the so-called "harder" part, when an order for medicine or a test is actually placed based on a doctor's diagnosis and recommendation.

The CISO emphasized that the Health Information Technology for Economic and Clinical Health (HITECH) Act,[5] by requiring doctors to use electronic order entry by 2015,[6] has inserted "medical IT" into the center or medical practice itself. The importance of this new requirement, he commented, can't be overstated.

- The CISO added that getting electronic order entry wrong could cause a doctor's life to go from "bad" to "intolerably bad." Specifically, he stated that some technologies already slow down trust delegation data processes used by doctors today. In view of the fast approaching 2015 deadline, he added, some doctors fear that faulty or underperforming order entry technology could compromise their already "brittle" medical record exchange systems. The CISO observed that doctors further worry that the new mandate will require them to do more work, slow them down, and ultimately reduce their productivity by cutting the total number of patients they can see on a daily basis. Given the already low reimbursement rates of Medicare and other programs, he concluded, this could result in severe risk to a health care organization's already low profit margins.

---

[5] The HITECH Act, enacted in Title XIII of the American Recovery and Reinvestment Act of 2009 (Pub.L. 111-5), set as a critical national goal the "meaningful use" of interoperable EHR. Wikipedia. Health Information Technology for Economic and Clinical Health Act. ONLINE. N.D. Available: http://en.wikipedia.org/wiki/Health_Information_Technology_for_Economic_and_Clinical_Health_Act [23 January 2014]. The term "meaningful use" means that health care providers use certified EHR technology in ways that can be measured significantly in quality and quantity. U.S. Department of Health and Human Services. ONLINE. N.D. Available: http://www.hrsa.gov/healthit/meaningfuluse/ [24 January 2014]. Under the HITECH Act, health care providers that achieved meaningful use by 2011 became eligible for incentive payments. Meaningful Use. ONLINE. N.D. Available: http://www.healthcareitnews.com/directory/meaningful-use [8 January 2014]. Those who fail to do so by 2015 may be penalized. *Id.* Stage 1 meaningful use criteria set the baseline for electronic data capture and information sharing, while Stage 2 and Stage 3 – expected to be implemented in 2015 – will continue to expand on that baseline. *Id.*

[6] Electronic order entry, also known as Computerized Physician Order Entry (CPOE), refers to a process of electronic entry of medical practitioner instructions for the treatment of patients (particularly hospitalized patients) under a physician's care. Wikipedia. Computerized Physician Order Entry. ONLINE. N.D. Available: http://en.wikipedia.org/wiki/Computerized_physician_order_entry [8 January 2014]. These orders are communicated over a computer network to the medical staff or to the departments (pharmacy, laboratory, or radiology) responsible for fulfilling the order. *Id.* CPOE is intended to decrease delay in order completion, reduce errors related to handwriting or transcription, allow order entry at the point of care or off-site, provide error-checking for duplicate or incorrect doses or tests, and simplify inventory and posting of charges. *Id.*

- When another IT professional responded that some of the challenges with adopting electronic order entry may arise from the preferences of individual doctors rather than from underlying sector dynamics, i.e., "people" problems versus "process" problems, the CISO disagreed. He stated that medical IT applications have always slowed doctors down, but that they typically complete only the documentation portion of the medical record exchange process – leaving order entry to other staff such as nurses, pharmacists, and other licensed professionals. Regardless of the technical preference of doctors, he added, the requirement that they now play a bigger role in the order entry process itself imposes a significant burden. The CISO concluded that doctors typically aren't technophobes but literally can't afford to be slowed down by anything at the patient point of care.

- The CISO remarked that the EHR solutions industry is comparatively immature, likening it to the maturity of enterprise resource planning (ERP) solutions in the 1980s and 1990s.[7] While massive changes in the EHR solutions industry are underway, he continued, obtaining the right solutions still can be very hard. He noted that integrating and obtaining required levels of interoperability among systems, based on existing Health Level Seven International (HL7) and other standards, present even more complex challenges that will require patience and tolerance by all relevant stakeholders as the health care sector evolves in the years ahead.

- The CISO then cited the overwhelming need for health care organizations to communicate both internally among their various business units and externally with other organizations in order to serve their patients. In view of the complex coordination this requires, he observed, it's not surprising that their medical record exchange systems are "brittle." "Securing brittle systems is very difficult," he added, and imposing new layers of security on them only contributes to their "brittleness." The CISO concluded that for these reasons, health care organizations generally are not predisposed to supporting major cybersecurity investments.

*REGULATORY REGIMES AND AUDITS*

*HIPAA*

- Despite these challenges, the CISO explained that cyber incidents nevertheless are very much on the radar of most health care organizations given the main regulatory structure against which they must perform: HIPAA. Although he described HIPAA as a law that's "difficult to decipher," he stated that health care organizations pay very close attention to the results of HIPAA audits in order to understand how the Department of Health and Human Services (HHS) assesses and evaluates cybersecurity best practices. The CISO disclosed that HHS recently subjected HCO 2 to

---

[7] Enterprise resource planning (ERP) software refers to business process management software that allows an organization to use a system of integrated applications to manage its business and automate back office functions. Webopedia. ERP – Enterprise Resource Planning. ONLINE. N.D. Available: http://www.webopedia.com/TERM/E/ERP.htm [14 January 2014]. ERP software integrates all facets of an organization's operation, including product planning, development, manufacturing processes, sales and marketing. *Id.*

a random HIPAA audit that provided it with a series of performance scores against a full range of HIPAA regulations.

- The CISO advised that pursuant to HIPAA, HHS publishes the results of investigations into security breach events that impact over 500 people. He added that there have been over 800 such incidents for which investigation results have been made publicly available – a list known in the trade as the "wall of shame." He stated that the most common source of reported HIPAA violations stems from the theft and/or loss of laptops and desktop computers, and that lost paper records run a close second. He noted that the number of health care organizations reporting hacking incidents also has ticked up, rising from very low percentages several years ago to the 10-12% range today. The CISO said that although only about 80 breaches in the last three to four years have involved over 500 people, many more are "almost certainly" occurring but go undetected. He concluded that these statistics nevertheless show that HIPAA is driving a more complete accounting of what were, until recently, undisclosed security lapses.

- The CISO added that even as health care organizations are seeing a rise in the number of reported laptop security breaches, they're also seeing a rise in the number of reported paper-based security breaches – e.g., hospitals failing to shred patient records and other documents properly, opening them to compromise by dumpster diving criminals. He asserted that this trend indicates that security breach reporting generally – driven by HIPAA and other authorities laws – is improving in terms of its pervasiveness and thoroughness.

*HIPAA's Limits*

- The CISO reported that his fundamental concern with HIPAA as a cybersecurity "regulation" is that it doesn't effectively address his biggest security problem: the malicious hacking of EHRs and the medical IT infrastructure that supports their creation, sharing, and storage. He observed that HIPAA instead focuses on securing the medical IT infrastructure that supports the business processes that enable doctors to see and treat their patients. While ensuring that those processes are "up and working" is important, he continued, that emphasis creates a perverse incentive to *not* focus on the cybersecurity of everything else. The CISO attributed this shortcoming to the sector's "mental model" of what constitutes a medical IT failure. "The community does not see IT as a vector for attack," he explained, "but rather as an enabler of organizational processes that themselves are often difficult to effectively perform." In short, health care organizations face stiff fines if they fail to comply with HIPAA's regulations concerning medical IT availability, so their leadership unsurprisingly directs the bulk of available security funding to that area.

- The CISO observed that cybersecurity professionals instinctively realize that conversion to an EHR system opens new opportunities for unauthorized access to, or corruption of, patient health records. This new vector of attack, he added, compounds the already significant challenges that exist with securing medical IT infrastructure – much of which health care organizations outsource to third parties in order to save money. "If a health care provider

18

doesn't even hire its own networking experts," he stated, "it's even less realistic to expect that it will hire its own security experts." The CISO added that HIPAA further complicates this situation. The law's emphasis on business process security, he added provides health care organizations with a further rationale to bypass the larger issue of ensuring network security altogether and focus instead on regulatory compliance. "In other words," he concluded, "those who can't and/or won't do security do compliance."

- The CISO advised that this HIPAA prism consequently makes his cyber risk management messaging to HCO 2 leadership very challenging. He explained that when HCO 2 leadership asks him how things are going with network security, he responds, "Everything is going great; the situation is dire." From a HIPAA perspective, he stated, the very few notification events (involving impacted business operations) that HCO 2 has experienced *is* great. By contrast, threats to the HCO 2 community's intellectual property (IP) and PII from malicious hackers, nation-states, and others pose very serious and growing problems.

- The CISO noted that efforts to gather data about malicious hacking incidents across the HCO 2 enterprise are relatively new and that discerning trends in this area is accordingly difficult. Consistent with HIPAA's business process-oriented regulations and related statistics, however, he confirmed that HCO 2's main "operational" security breaches stem from the theft and/or loss of laptops and desktops. Publication of sensitive data on the Internet, he added, represents an additional challenge area.

## REGULATORY REGIMES AND AUDITS QUESTIONS

- The CISO's discussion about HIPAA – and the theft and/or loss of laptops and desktops in particular – spurred a series of questions from other roundtable participants about academic freedom, how HCO 2 conducts its asset management activities, and what software solutions it uses for those activities.

### ACADEMIC FREEDOM

- An insurer asked why laptops aren't encrypted as a matter of course if they represent the leading cause of security breaches. The CISO responded that the number of unencrypted HCO 2 laptops has decreased significantly in recent years but that the BYOD trend has driven up the number of personal laptops in use on HCO 2's network. He advised that the reason for this development is straightforward: medical researchers expect to be able to use their personal laptops and open-source software to conduct their work in collaboration with others. Taking away their permission to do so, he stated, would not only severely restrict their ability to conduct research but also run counter to the very concept of academic freedom. "The freedom to compute," he concluded, "is fundamental to conducting science." Unfortunately, he added, some researchers forget to enable the encryption installed on their personal laptops when exercising that freedom.

- The CISO advised, moreover, that significant problems arise when conducting network device interrogations to remotely verify whether the encryption software on personal laptops connected to the HCO 2 network is operating. He explained that those myriad personal laptops used by both medical researchers and doctors – often for very different purposes – include many different kinds of encryption software. This variation could well lead to incomplete or inconsistent interrogation results that, in turn, would require significant follow up with and inconvenience for end users.

- The CISO observed that while HCO 2 can attempt to reduce unnecessary data, monitor the data that leaves its major warehouses, and institute reasonable security practices for people to follow, it remains severely limited in its ability to address many cyber risks given its academic culture. For this reason, he advised, rules-based security efforts such as whitelisting are wholly unviable within the HCO 2 environment. He added that the biggest related issue on the horizon is with network permissions – specifically, balancing end user freedom to access whatever networks they deem necessary for research with the very real security threats that attach to some of those networks. The CISO stated that HCO 2 will likely continue to err on the side of academic freedom when faced with a tradeoff between openness and security.

- The CISO concluded that while the profile of malicious hacking incidents that target PII continues to rise, significant changes to the academic mindset about cybersecurity won't happen until end users experience first-hand the consequences of a cyber incident. He advised that those changes might come about as a result of browser exploits such as ransomware and keyboard loggers that negatively affect the ability of end users to perform online banking and other personal tasks on their organizations' networks. In his view, once end users become more suspicious about the cybersecurity of their workplaces, they'll become more open to network owners implementing the kinds of security improvements that they currently resist.

*ASSET MANAGEMENT AND SOFTWARE SECURITY SOLUTIONS*

- An IT professional noted that many organizations don't have a complete understanding of where their electronic assets are located and, as a result, must resort to managing assets in an indirect fashion by issuing device calls to identify asset matches. The CISO agreed, noting that the BYOD trend, for instance, makes visibility into devices connecting into the network more difficult. He added, however, that he isn't surprised by the current lack of clear asset management procedures – especially because the networks to which assets connect often comprise multiple smaller, federated networks. The CISO explained that HCO 2 occasionally acquires medical facilities that have existing networks of their own and then absorbs those legacy networks into its community network. As an example, he described a hospital that once maintained a wireless network with very strict access permission rules. Those rules had worked because the hospital had hosted only five or six devices as compared to the 50,000 devices on the HCO 2 network. With its addition to the HCO 2 community, however, it was required to adopt HCO 2's wireless rules. While the hospital now enjoys the benefits of easier provisioning through HCO 2's community network, its accordant cyber risks have substantially increased.

- An insurer then advised that he worked with a client that once employed an IT professional who downloaded a health care IT database onto a jump drive, took it home to work on his personal laptop, and then uploaded it back on his work computer – all without any malicious intention. Years later, the individual sold his personal laptop at a second-hand store. The person who bought it found the sensitive information and offered to return it to the client for $10,000. The insurer asked how HCO 2 protects itself against this type of risk. The CISO replied that to chase down incidents like this one, health care organizations would need an impossibly huge staff. Accordingly, they must accept some level of data breach vulnerability as residual risk because health care data is the lifeblood of their businesses operations. He explained that if rules make it too difficult to move data around, even in the name of security, the efficiency of an entire organization will be compromised and service standards will degrade accordingly.

- A second insurer asked if HCO 2 is using data loss prevention (DLP) software to monitor information downloaded onto removable media.[8] The CISO responded that HCO 2 is beginning to successfully use DLP software for e-mail and device-based checking. He advised, however, that implementing DLP software for network-based checks and monitoring traffic exiting the HCO 2 network remains difficult given the sheer amount of data that it must examine. The CISO explained that that DLP software allows health care organizations to see patient data on almost all of its many machines – to such an extent that they're "swimming in data." Under those circumstances, he stated, it can be very challenging to determine what type of indicator should even trigger a DLP event. The CISO advised that he's consequently pushing HCO 2 to adopt an enterprise desktop encryption policy to better address network-level data loss.

- An IT professional next asked about the utility of Database Activity Monitoring (DAM),[9] which monitors, captures, and records database events in near real-time and provides alerts about information policy violations. The CISO replied that DAM can be useful for mitigating data breach risks but that even DAM processes many not provide sufficient clarity into the activities that are happening "at their source." He stated that thoroughly exploring all questionable

---

[8] Data loss prevention (DLP) refers to systems that detect potential data breach and/or exfiltration transmissions and prevent them by monitoring, detecting, and blocking sensitive data while in-use (endpoint actions), in-motion (network traffic), and at-rest (data storage). Wikipedia. Data Loss Prevention Software. ONLINE. N.D. Available: http://en.wikipedia.org/wiki/Data_loss_prevention_software [15 January 2014].

[9] Database Activity Monitoring (DAM) refers to the observation of actions in a database. SearchITChannel. Database Activity Monitoring (DAM). ONLINE. N.D. Available: http://searchitchannel.techtarget.com/definition/database-activity-monitoring-DAM [11 January 2014]. DAM can be accomplished through a combination of several methods, including network sniffing, reading of database audit logs and/or system tables and memory scraping. *Id.* Regardless of the methodology chosen, the data must be correlated in order to detect and get a more accurate picture of what's going on within the database. *Id.*

database events requires a significant amount of analytical manpower – a dedicated use of resources that most health care organizations, including HCO 2, cannot afford.

## HCO 2 RISK MANAGEMENT CULTURE

### GOVERNANCE

- The CISO stated that HCO 2 is not organized like a conventional business but rather as a federation of approximately 8,000 small businesses. That construct, he continued, contains a multitude of individual research protocols and features leaders in each of those small businesses who exercise significant levels of autonomy. Simply protecting sensitive information across those many entities, he stated, is a sufficiently challenging problem. His job as a security specialist therefore is to try to convince everyone to "row in the same [security] direction."

- The CISO advised that given this environment, the HCO 2 board does not exercise as much centralized control in practice as do the boards of for-profit companies. Even if HCO 2 board members had such control, however, his ability to communicate cyber risks to them is further complicated by the highly technical nature of most cybersecurity problems. It can be very difficult to clearly define the boundaries of what constitutes information security in the health care sector, he observed, and justifying priorities to leadership accordingly becomes very challenging.

- The CISO then referenced HCO 2's IT strategy to describe how and where cybersecurity is prioritized within the HCO 2 community. That strategy, he said, focuses on five core concepts: (1) functionality; (2) usability; (3) portability/extensibility/interoperability (highlighting interoperability among systems); (4) resilience; and (5) security. HCO 2 essentially divides 100% of its IT budget five ways, he explained, with each division receiving a 20% share. The CISO added (happily) that "because resilience and security work together," he ends up with 40% of the resources. He concluded that while the IT strategy is not a security strategy, it nevertheless helps explain HCO 2's overall priorities and allocation of resources.

### STRATEGIES FOR SUCCESS

- The CISO reported that HCO 2 does not have a single cybersecurity strategy but instead "different strategies for different components of [HCO 2's] security efforts." He emphasized that the gap between strategy and tactics is consequently narrower for HCO 2 than in other entities given its construct as "a federation of multiple quasi-independent organizations." To illustrate his point, the CISO explained that he used to work individually with each HCO 2 business unit on its particular cybersecurity needs. That became overwhelming. Now, he stated, it's more effective and efficient to simply "watch the data." If he sees data leaving a major warehouse, he continued, he looks to where it's sent and then pushes more responsible security practices out to the entire HCO 2 community in order to collectively address the underlying issue.

- The CISO stressed his ongoing need to clearly communicate the pervasiveness of cyber risks to HCO 2 leadership in order to refine and mature the organization's existing risk management structures and to manage them more effectively. "When you have a culture that is structured to provide maximum benefit for science," he observed, "there's going to be an information security downside." The CISO advised that he hasn't gotten very far by focusing just on security risks and their potential impact on HCO 2's reputation. Instead, he stated, he focuses primarily on *compliance* risks and their potential impact on HCO 2's reputation. He explained that this framing through HIPAA enables him to focus on contrasts between risk management efforts. For example, he can draw distinctions between comprehensive ERM programs that other health care organizations have developed with the more modest DLP software and other solutions that HCO 2 has implemented. The CISO asserted that when he's able to demonstrate that other major competitors and peers take advantage of advanced risk management steps, he's more likely to receive funding to perform similar work.

- The CISO mentioned that this approach to securing funding is more effective in his environment than explicitly linking his cybersecurity resources requests to HCO 2's overall risk management strategy, which tends to develop through a very slow-moving and bureaucratic process. He stated that he instead "improvises" to fix problems. Focusing tactically on compliance risks that arise in the day-to-day environment, he added, has proven a highly successful way to obtain the cybersecurity funding he needs. "If we need to develop software and defeat hackers," he explained, "we do it and there's no need for the fanfare of a strategy to do it." He added that he nevertheless tries to link to "whatever strategy is in the works at the time" as a starting point before using tactics to actually fix the problems at hand. The CISO noted, however, that this approach makes it harder for him to translate HCO 2's current cybersecurity needs into strategic terms.

- The CISO advised that to support this approach, he and his team maintain "scorecards" that reflect cyber incident counts across the HCO 2 community. In the eyes of his leadership, he explained, the decreasing numbers of HIPAA notification events over recent years show that his efforts have been fairly effective. He acknowledged, however, that his tactics address only the tip of the iceberg – i.e., for compliance-based risk management purposes only – and that malicious hacker risks to EHRs and their supporting IT technology continue to escalate. The CISO asserted that, going forward, HCO 2 leadership must look beyond regulations-based cyber investments in order to better address growing risks from these and other threat sources.

- The CISO reported that one area where he has had some strategic success is with the HCO 2 workforce. He stated that he's told human resource personnel that under the surface, cyber risk is the greatest risk HCO 2 faces. He accordingly collaborates with the HCO 2 human resources department to try to modify the risk culture itself – through training opportunities and other initiatives – rather than address cyber risks by technical means alone (e.g., making the compliance risk case for encrypting more laptops). He reported that he's seen progress among cyber risk professionals across the HCO 2 community as a result of this engagement but that communication of cyber risk to top-level leadership remains difficult.

- When asked by a risk manager what "carrots" he uses to encourage more cybersecurity investment across HCO 2, the CISO quipped that his approach is to "stab leadership and security officers with the carrot" – that is, he highlights the negative ramifications (e.g., fines, public shaming) for non-compliance with HIPAA and ties as much of his security agenda as possible to existing compliance requirements. He did cite one incentive, however, that he routinely discusses with cybersecurity professionals who work on the medical research side of the HCO 2 enterprise: the Federal Information Security Management Act (FISMA).[10] The CISO explained that he tells his colleagues that investing in IT infrastructure to satisfy FISMA requirements makes it marginally easier to apply for future grants from the Federal Government. This marginal value, he asserted, may increase over time and further justify the investment.

*COMPLIANCE VERSUS ENTERPRISE RISK MANAGEMENT*

*COSTS, BENEFITS, AND THE POWER OF COMPLIANCE*

- An IT professional challenged the CISO's described approach to risk management, claiming that absent an enterprise risk-based approach to cybersecurity investment, HCO 2 will continually fall behind rapidly evolving cyber threats. A critical infrastructure representative concurred, noting that, "Strategy is not grand planning but the ability to step into board meetings, present a refined elevator pitch, and apply actions to the basic principles outlined in that pitch." The representative advised that he uses three words as the foundation of that elevator pitch – aggregate, automate, and accelerate – that lie at the root of his organization's operations. He then observed that risk management strategy is not so much about deploying tools as it is about helping people understand risk issues.

- The CISO responded that he runs a risk-based security program, albeit with compliance risk as its starting point, and that he too uses three words in his own pitches to HCO 2 leadership for funding – "see, segment, and spend." While he attempts to reduce investments involved in each category, he added, he's not overly focused on reducing costs because he's not yet come to the point where he's not getting the money he requests. The CISO acknowledged HCO 2's longer-term need to move beyond HIPAA-based cybersecurity investments but added that those investments will come over time once his leadership comes to understand the full range of cyber risks that HCO 2 faces.

- A risk manager then asked how the CISO uses cost/benefit considerations to inform his cybersecurity investment portfolio. He replied that he and his team have developed a series of metrics based on what it will cost the organization in terms of HIPAA fines if specific cyber incidents occur without appropriate controls being in place. Put simply, he advised, he's

---

[10] The Federal Information Security Management Act of 2002 (44 U.S.C. § 3541, et seq.) was enacted in 2002 as Title III of the E-Government Act of 2002 (Pub.L. 107-347, 116 Stat. 2899).

developed a cost avoidance structure that helps him highlight specific actions that HCO 2 should take now to completely avoid or otherwise mitigate losses. "My approach," he continued, "is to tell my leadership the following: when the HIPAA cops come in and turn over all the tables and find other things as a result of this breach, this is what we're likely to pay in fines; if we do these five things, we'll likely reduce the fines by X amount." This approach works, he added, because it's often too difficult to predict other losses associated with a breach (e.g., the value of lost IP).

- The CISO concluded that while HIPAA accordingly might not help him address "freak breaches" – that is, the kinds of breaches that a more strategic approach might anticipate – the fines that arise from HIPAA compliance failures are something his leadership immediately understands. In short, HIPAA serves as a powerful tool to justify at least a subset of very worthy cybersecurity investments. The CSO nevertheless lamented that HIPAA does not better address cyber risks more generally given its role as HCO 2's primary driver of IT security funding.

## COSTS, BENEFITS, AND ENTERPRISE APPROACHES

- An IT professional asked whether HCO 2 hosts a cross-domain committee to examine and address cyber risks on an enterprise level. The CISO replied that although such a committee once existed, it ultimately failed because "it didn't sign the checks."

- An insurer responded that, in a highly federated system such as the HCO 2 community, establishing a cross-functional risk management group comprised of senior representatives from HCO 2's many business units would be helpful. He stated that such a group could help those representatives explain what cyber risk "costs" – not to the entire HCO 2 enterprise but to the individual HCO 2 business units themselves. Using such a structure, he advised, would empower the HCO 2 business units to self-identify and address the cyber risks of greatest importance to them. The CISO agreed in theory but emphasized that cyber risk mitigation comes with an institutional cost in the health care context. He explained that HIPAA regulations do not apply to HCO 2's individual business units but to the organization as a whole. He added that HCO 2 consequently has been working to bring all its cyber risk management activities within a single, organization-wide cost/benefit analysis. He described that analysis as one that is significantly more mature today than ten years ago. The CISO then explained (again) that what drives that analysis are the follow-on costs of a cyber incident – that is, the total fines that will be imposed upon HCO 2 *organizationally* as a result of a HIPAA violation.

- A second insurer asked if a cross-functional group would work better if it was allowed to "sign checks" – that is, integrate cyber into the overall incentives structure of the organization in order to motivate change. The CISO responded that he doubted this approach would succeed – not only for the reasons previously stated but also given the likely difficulties involved with incentivizing the vast number of end users within the HCO 2 environment. He explained that given their sheer number of doctors, students, and others within that environment, taking cybersecurity all the way down to the individual level would be tough. "We should do a better job of changing end user behavior," he acknowledged, "but we're not at a mature enough level to do this yet."

- The insurer then asked if the CISO's calculus would change if a cross-functional group was empowered to sign checks to cover things beyond technology expenditures, including insurance and public relations efforts. The CISO replied that he could justify such expenditures already through his team's HIPAA compliance efforts.

*REGULATION*

- A risk manager commented that HCO 2's risk culture appears to be "slowing its progress toward meaningfully addressing cyber risks," and asked if cybersecurity regulation beyond HIPAA could help drive improvements. He specifically referenced regulatory actions in the financial sector that have helped companies to internalize cyber risks posed by malicious hackers and others by providing them with a binary choice: compliance or non-compliance. The risk manager observed that catastrophic risk models of cyber and other incidents often do not resonate with organizational leadership in the financial sector because of their inherent ambiguity – in other words, even mature catastrophic risk models cannot effectively demonstrate that a company will be driven out of business by a given catastrophic event. On the other hand, he continued, leadership knows that regulatory non-compliance can very quickly put a bank out of business. This realization, he concluded, often motivates immediate action on the cybersecurity front.

- The CISO replied that cybersecurity-focused regulatory authorities have indeed driven high levels of compliance within the IT security community generally but not as heavily within the health care community. He reiterated, however, that all research performed by HCO 2 on behalf of the Federal Government is subject to FISMA and NIST 800-53 security regulations and requirements. As a result, he noted, those authorities have been a "huge" driver for enhanced cybersecurity on the medical research side of the HCO 2 enterprise. The CISO advised that herding the FISMA and NIST 800-53 compliance efforts of multiple business units within even this more discrete area, however, presents ongoing and significant challenges.

- An insurer asked the CISO if the concept of meaningful use, as defined in the HITECH Act is also driving his efforts.[11] The CISO responded affirmatively, explaining that the meaningful use paradigm now requires him to consider the security of data at-rest in addition to data in-motion. He asserted that this will invariably lead to a strategic requirement to encrypt entire databases, adding that he'd "love" to be able to reference a current law or regulation to justify such action. In the meantime, the CISO concluded, real-time security issues that impact the delivery of medical services continue to dominate his responsibility set and accordingly require the bulk of his funding resources.

---

[11] *See* HITECH Act "meaningful use" definition, *supra* note 5.

- A critical infrastructure representative from another health care organization noted that his institution faces many of the same cultural challenges and issues as HCO 2 when it comes to motivating senior leadership to take action against cyber risks. He reported that his board members also struggle to meaningfully manage end-user behavior in addition to the architecture-related cyber risks that the CISO described. The representative added that his board members have only a limited understanding about where their organization "stacks up" against existing security models. Unlike the HCO 2 board, he asserted, reputational and safety risks nevertheless are huge issues for his board and have motivated several deep dives into his organization's broader cyber risk management practices. These deep dives, he observed, have resulted in the creation of severa cybersecurity investment strategies. The representative concluded that his organization therefore appears to be less motivated by news of individual HIPAA breaches than is apparently the case at HCO 2.

- A social scientist then asked if any risk management processes broadly address cyber-related reputational risks. He suggested that such processes must be more complex than simply addressing compliance issues and instead might include such areas as investment relations, crisis management, and the like. An insurer replied that a primary consideration for health care and other organizations should be mitigating exposure to reputational risk and that they should not limit the scope of their incident response activity to just regulatory compliance. The social scientist agreed, noting that crisis management communications were particularly essential. "There's a significant difference between proactively disclosing that an organization had one major cyber incident during a given year," he stated, "and responding to a negative article about a cyber incident in the New York Times." The social scientist added that reputational losses can easily trump business fines.

- The CISO responded that although HCO 2 does face reputational risks for security breaches – and has suffered related losses in the past – the potential costs for failing to comply with HIPAA are, in many respects, worse. He then presented a hypothetical about a patient with a strange, life-threatening disease whose doctor says he's going to put the patient's EHRs on a CD and hand it out to everyone in Times Square. Despite this threatened breach of privacy, he continued, the patient still will say to the doctor, "Treat me." The CISO observed that this sums up where the health care sector is focused when it comes to cybersecurity: on securing medical IT to ensure effective patient treatment rather than the security of patient data.

## HCO 2 USE CASE

### THE INCIDENT

- The CISO described a cyber incident at HCO 2 that involved malicious hackers who inserted malware via Structured Query Language (SQL) injection through a web interface that was used to control an electron microscope in a student lab.[12] The malware caused several HCO 2 network servers to beacon out to various bad overseas Internet Protocol (IP) addresses. The incursions affected an administrator account, and the CISO accordingly contacted the server administrator – a non-central IT participant – to alert him to the problem. That individual subsequently checked his systems' diagnostics and blocked the bad IP addresses. After taking over the server that controlled the web interface, the malicious hackers had apparently waited to see what other servers communicated with it. In so doing, they compromised a total of 30 servers with the same administrator account.

- The malicious hackers had kept a low profile in order to access as much information from employee credentials as possible. The CISO stated that it wasn't clear how much agency was involved in the attack but speculated that it could have been highly automated. As a result, the incursion may not have been as aggressively exploratory as it might otherwise have been. The CISO explained that his concern was less about the disruption of applications and more about the addition of unauthorized and undesired functionality on the HCO 2 network. On the contrary, none of the organization's applications had been disrupted to the point of causing financial loss. Cleaning up the infected machines, however, posed a major challenge because the malicious hackers had been able to move around quickly among multiple machines.

*USE CASE IMPLICATIONS*

- The CISO described this and incidents like it as typical within the health care sector and stated that most go unnoticed because any associated loss of functionality is rare. He explained that the bad IP addresses involved in this use case, however, had fortuitously been published in a threat alert bulletin from the REN-ISAC. An analyst on his team who happened upon the bulletin while reviewing his email plugged in the addresses and found the problem. The CISO added that while HCO 2 eventually would have discovered the beaconing activity when it performed its routine network scans, the information sharing by the REN-ISAC combined with the diligence of the analyst brought about a much quicker fix.

- The CISO explained that the use case incident underscores the fact that health care organizations are just as much targets of malicious cyber actors as are defense contractors and other more "in the news" organizations. This kind of event, he added, demonstrates in stark terms HIPAA's shortcomings when it comes to motivating effective cyber risk management investment against malicious hackers.

---

[12] Structured Query Language (SQL) injection refers to an attack technique that attempts to subvert the relationship between a webpage and its supporting database, typically in order to trick the database into executing malicious code. United States Computer Emergency Readiness Team (US-CERT). SQL Injection. ONLINE. June 22, 2012. Available: http://www.us-cert.gov/security-publications/sql-injection [29 January 2014]. SQL injection usually involves a combination of "overelevated" permissions, unsanitized/untyped user input, and/or true software (database) vulnerabilities. *Id*. Since SQL injection is possible even when no traditional software vulnerabilities exist, mitigation is often much more complicated than simply applying a security patch. *Id*.

- The CISO reiterated his concern that organizations such as HCO 2 focus primarily – and almost exclusively – on the fines they face for failing to comply with HIPAA rather than the larger cybersecurity picture. Malicious hackers may be actively trolling their networks in an effort to exfiltrate IP data, he continued, but they'll never know it because they're not incentivized to proactively find and remove them. He concluded that without evolving beyond their currently excessive focus on compliance, health care organizations may be in for rough days ahead.

## CYBERSECURITY INSURANCE

- The CISO explained that HCO 2 maintains cybersecurity insurance with very high deductibles for some data breach risks. He noted, however, that HCO 2 has never been compensated for a cyber incident, so the "real limits" of what its policies cover have not undergone a real-world test. The CISO advised that he engages with insurance underwriters as part of his job duties and doesn't "pull punches" by withholding detailed information about the kinds of incidents that HCO 2 has experienced and the additional risks it faces. He added, however, that he doesn't have a high degree of confidence that HCO 2's cyber insurance will fully cover the costs of an actual cyber incident. He nevertheless believes that cybersecurity insurance is worth having given its *potential* for coverage.

## HEALTH CARE ORGANIZATION 3

<u>ORGANIZATION OVERVIEW:</u>   The Risk Management Director (RMD) and Global Operations Center Director (GOCD) for Health Care Organization 3 (HCO 3) described HCO 3 as a medical vendor comprised of three major divisions:  health care consumer products, pharmaceuticals, and medical devices/technology. Each division, they advised, is responsible for its own research and development, corporate sales, and supply chain management activities, including risk management activities.  The RMD further characterized HCO 3 as a "highly federated and distributed international enterprise" that includes 260 operating companies located in some 60 countries.  "We have a decentralized management approach," he noted, "with eggs in 260 baskets."  To illustrate his point, the RMD referenced the fact that approximately 150 of HCO 3's operating companies host their own ERP software platforms.[13]  He remarked that this is a bit more than even HCO 3 can bear, and that it recently initiated a standardization program to bring the platforms under a "single management set" in order to promote greater efficiencies.

The RMD asserted that cyber attacks are less likely to affect the entire HCO 3 organization given its highly federated and distributed nature.  The company accordingly doesn't maintain fully centralized security operations – employing just 350 people in that category, of whom only 50-60 focus on information security.  The RMD explained that only a small number of those professionals work on "true" cybersecurity.  "We only do [cyber risk] analysis when we're tipped off," he observed.  "While we're moving from a reactionary to a 'pro-actionary' approach, from a corporate perspective we need to fight day-to-day fires to keep [HCO 3] operations up and running."

The GOCD added that to support this tactical battle rhythm, he manages a strategic operations center staffed with a "total incident response team" that responds to all business critical outages that impact HCO 3's worldwide operations.  "If a server is down and we're not making hip replacements," he stated, "we're losing $100,000 an hour."  The GOCD advised that he's deployed a number of staff internationally to support his team's efforts.

<u>USE CASE PRESENTATION AND DISCUSSION:</u>

*CYBER RISK LANDSCAPE*

- The RMD reported that HCO 3 rarely sells products and services directly to consumers, a business model that effectively transfers a significant amount of cyber risk to its outsourced providers and intermediaries.  He observed that this arrangement makes HCO 3 a somewhat "different kind of animal" than some of its competitors.  The RMD nevertheless described the company's priority risk as "product safety."  While the majority of HCO 3's customers are medical professionals or medical enterprises, he added, the company must ensure that its risk management efforts remain focused on the ultimate consumer:  individuals who directly use or are otherwise treated with HCO 3's products.

---

[13] *See* ERP definition, *supra* note 7.

- The RMD explained that companies like HCO 3 face complex challenges in implementing security policies across their multiple divisions, numerous operating companies, and myriad business units. For example, he continued, different consumers within the same industry sector might use a HCO 3 technology for very different purposes. That same technology, in turn, could be marketed for all those and additional purposes in still other industry sectors. That's where things get complicated from a cyber risk management standpoint. The RMD advised that each HCO 3 technology carries with it varying IT security requirements depending upon its intended use. The widely varying and sheer number of those intended uses – within and across industry sectors – makes standardization of security policies for vended technologies very difficult.

- The RMD noted that another source of HCO 3 cyber risk stems from the fact that its major growth drivers are emerging medical markets in developing nations. Many of those nations, he commented, do not have the underlying infrastructure necessary to implement the full scope of IT requirements that would be expected of medical vendors in developed countries. He specifically mentioned in this regard the infeasibility of bringing an ERP software platform into medical markets in China, Malaysia, and Vietnam.[14] He then stated that ROI considerations present still another obstacle. "We can't justify taking [an ERP software platform] that costs $100 million to operate annually into a developing market," he observed, "when we generate only $2 million in revenue there annually."

- The RMD explained that yet another obstacle to HCO 3's cyber risk management efforts arises from the highly varied legal, security (i.e., employee safety), and other compliance requirements that exist within the multiple international, state, and local jurisdictions in which the company operates. He advised that HCO 3 works hard to harmonize its security and other compliance requirements through a unified Governance, Risk Management, and Compliance (GRC) platform,[15] but that disparities among its host jurisdictions significantly complicate its efforts. He explained that HCO 3 nevertheless requires all of its operating companies to address four overarching risk categories, regardless of their geographic location:

  o Strategic Risk. HCO 3's strategic risk assessments focus on the loss of IP, especially in so-called "grey markets."[16]

---

[14] *Id.*

[15] The term "GRC platform" or "GRC software" refers to software that allows publicly-held companies to integrate and manage IT operations that are subject to regulation. TechTarget.com. GRC (Governance, Risk Management, Compliance) Software. ONLINE. 3 May 2010. Available: http://searchcio.techtarget.com/definition/GRC-governance-risk-management-and-compliance-software [21 January 2014]. Such software typically combines applications that manage the core functions of GRC into a single integrated package. *Id.* GRC software enables an organization to pursue a systematic, organized approach to managing GRC-related strategy and implementation. *Id.* Instead of keeping data in separate "silos," administrators can use a single framework to monitor and enforce rules and procedures. *Id.* Successful installations enable organizations to manage risk, reduce costs incurred by multiple installations and minimize complexity for managers. *Id.*

[16] The term "grey market" refers to a market where a product is bought and sold outside the manufacturer's authorized trading channels. Investopedia. Grey Market. ONLINE. N.D. Available: http://www.investopedia.com/terms/g/greymarket.asp [14 January 2014]. For example, if a store owner is an

- o Operational Risk. HCO 3's operational risk assessments focus on disruption to product supply; physical damage and disruption; and the confidentiality, integrity, and availability of IT resources. HCO 3's primary concern among these categories is the availability of IT resources because the company can't make money if its systems aren't operating.

- o Compliance Risk. HCO 3's compliance risk management efforts focus on global regulation, including but not limited to regulations that pertain to cybersecurity, employee health, patient safety, clinical trials, and tax policy.

- o Financial and Reporting Risk. HCO 3's financial and reporting risk management efforts focus on ensuring compliance with relevant reporting requirements. In the wake of the Sarbanes-Oxley Act, the company places an increasingly high priority on enhancing its reporting processes.[17]

- The RMD explained that for all four of these overarching risk categories, each HCO 3 operating company tailors its related policies, processes, and programs to address the specific circumstances and unique requirements of its host jurisdiction.

- Regarding the "Financial and Reporting Risk" category, the RMD warned that the greater emphasis on reporting requirements occasioned by the Sarbanes-Oxley Act has the potential to complicate the actual security posture of public companies by "unintentionally turning security programs into compliance programs." The RMD asserted that HCO 3 accordingly works actively to counteract this potential drift.

*HCO 3 RISK MANAGEMENT CULTURE*

*GOVERNANCE*

- The RMD stated that despite the highly varied environments in which HCO 3 does business, he nevertheless establishes uniform corporate policies that apply to all of its operating companies in several key areas such as digital asset risk management and internal IT control adoption. With the blessing of the HCO 3 board of directors, he then "pushes out" those policies for implementation. The RMD added that HCO 3 hosts a number of audit and compliance

---

unauthorized dealer of a certain high-end electronics brand, the product is considered to be sold on the grey market. *Id.*

[17] The Sarbanes–Oxley Act of 2002 (Pub.L. 107–204, 116 Stat. 745, enacted July 30, 2002) , also known as Sarbanes–Oxley, Sarbox or SOX, is a United States federal law that set new or enhanced standards for all U.S. public company boards, management, and public accounting firms. Wikipedia. Sarbanes-Oxley Act. ONLINE. N.D. Available: http://en.wikipedia.org/wiki/Sarbanes%E2%80%93Oxley_Act [15 January 2014]. Under the law, top management must now individually certify the accuracy of financial information. *Id.* In addition, penalties for fraudulent financial activity are much more severe. *Id.* The law likewise increases the independence of outside auditors who review the accuracy of corporate financial statements and increases the oversight role of boards of directors. *Id.*

committees that have direct access to the board to assist in this regard, superseding the CEO in certain circumstances. For example, he continued, all business risk matters and "damage to public trust" issues – no matter where they arise globally – go directly to the board for review and action.

- The RMD advised that to bring cohesion to its overall risk management process, HCO 3 hosts an enterprise risk management council (ERM Council) to better understand and address risks that arise across the company. He explained that HCO 3 established the ERM Council only after agreeing to do so as part of a lawsuit settlement agreement. While pursuing an ERM strategy was the right thing to do anyway, he observed, the lawsuit underscored for everyone the importance of pursuing proactive approaches to risk management.

*STRATEGIES FOR SUCCESS*

*ERM FRAMEWORKS*

- The RMD reported that HCO 3's health care consumer products, pharmaceuticals, and medical devices/technology divisions have all adopted and use their own ERM Frameworks to identify and assess their external and internal risks. While those frameworks reflect the specific business lines in question, and are informed by each division's available funding, business plan, and ERP solution, all share the following five process steps:

  o Identify and address external and internal risk. This step includes assessing the impacts of an event, system vulnerabilities, and environmental threats to the division.

  o Determine an appropriate risk response. This step represents the strategy "piece" of the ERM process, where decisions are made on how best to allocate technological solutions, programmatic controls, and human resources for the division's benefit.

  o Establish policies and procedures to support the risk response. This step includes the division's development of accountability structures, internal testing, programmatic controls, and response systems – and/or the adoption of well-established response guidance in the form of handbooks, policies, and other documents – to support risk response. Those documents may include scripts for explaining why an operating company within a division presents a particular risk and/or requires a certain risk control.

  o Communicate risks and establish mitigation plans. This step involves ensuring board visibility into a division's risks and related risk management efforts; establishing a business case for those efforts; and obtaining funding and other support for them.

  o Monitor risk program efficacy continuously.

- The RMD commented that for each of these steps, technology investment represents only one part of the risk management equation, which also includes people and process. HCO 3 consequently sponsors employee awareness programs, for example, to highlight processes that can address incidents effectively. The goal, he stated, is to instill knowledge about cyber risks and personal accountability for addressing them across the entire enterprise.

- A critical infrastructure representative asked the RMD if anyone working at HCO 3 has, in their performance review, a requirement for creating a controlled environment for HCO 3's multiple ERM Frameworks. The RMD responded affirmatively, noting that his own performance review includes the stipulation that he "maintain a controlled environment."

*CATASTROPHE PLANNING*

- The GOCD explained what would happen if HCO 3 were to experience a catastrophic event that required a major risk management decision such as shutting down operations at a key manufacturing plant. He advised that HCO 3 has developed a "run book" that designates a corporate emergency response team known as a "C-CERT" to convene and begin managing the incident response immediately. Depending upon the kind and duration of the event, he added, C-CERT members might include human resources, legal, operations, public relations, and other personnel. The GOCD reported that HCO 3 has not yet run a cyber exercise to test the run book but has scheduled one in the near future.

- The RMD added that the run book includes HCO 3's formal escalation policy for engaging the right company leadership at the right time. He explained that even without being exercised, the "relevant people [already] know their roles" during a variety of event scenarios and have received related training for them through HCO 3's extensive learning management system. The RMD noted that although he and the GOCD have a direct line to the CEO, they would follow the run book protocol regarding when and under what circumstances to contact him during an emergency situation.

## HCO 3 USE CASE

*THE INCIDENT*

- The GOCD described a cyber incident at HCO 3 that involved the CryptoLocker virus.[18] During the incident, malicious hackers obtained illicit access to two company laptops and mapped their drives. The malicious hackers then encrypted files stored on the drives. When HCO 3 employees logged onto the laptops, a pop-up box appeared stating, "You have to pay $400 if you want to access your files." While the mapping didn't extend to business critical files, the

---

[18] CryptoLocker is a new variant of ransomware that restricts access to infected computers and demands the victim provide a payment to the attackers in order to decrypt and recover their files. United States Computer Emergency Readiness Team (US-CERT). CryptoLocker Ransomware Infections. ONLINE. Nov. 18, 2013. Available: https://www.us-cert.gov/ncas/alerts/TA13-309A [14 January 2014]. The primary means of infection appears to be phishing emails containing malicious attachments. *Id.*

GOCD explained that the situation would have been "mission critical" had it done so. Even with the contained impact of this particular event, he noted, his team still had to restore approximately 5,000 files from backup tapes.

## INCIDENT OBSERVATIONS

- The GOCD emphasized the importance of bringing response teams into strategic discussions when addressing real-time, unfolding events like the CryptoLocker incident. The perspectives of those teams, he advised, are essential for determining what an event actually means to a business and how it should be addressed over the long term.

- The RMD added that cyber risk management cultures vary from company to company depending upon the nature of their business. Given HCO 3's emphasis on maintaining the availability of operations across its three business divisions, he continued, HCO 3 has prioritized a risk management process that's highly reactive to incidents like the one described in the use case.

## USE CASE QUESTIONS

## COST/BENEFIT COMMUNICATIONS TO LEADERSHIP

## RISK MANAGEMENT ROADMAPS

- A critical infrastructure representative observed that the CryptoLocker incident was not a catastrophic or otherwise corporate-wide event. He then asked how HCO 3 nevertheless could "use it" to both inform and justify risk-based investments to the board. The GOCD responded that his team meets monthly with HCO 3's Chief Technology Officer (CTO) to review significant security incidents and to determine what mitigation and controls to apply in response. He advised that HCO 3 has a well-established cyber risk management cycle that includes a lengthy list of cyber incidents that might impact the company and corresponding mitigations and controls that are specifically "road-mapped" to address them. When reviewing a significant cyber incident, he continued, the CTO will determine the urgency of executing an applicable road-mapped solution or a new one if necessary. The GOCD added that if an unforeseen cyber incident is sufficiently serious, the CTO can amend the incident list to include it and its corresponding mitigations and controls for future reference.

- The GOCD advised that this cyber risk management cycle directly informs how new cyber incidents are communicated to the board for action. "Depending on the need," he stated, "we can escalate a request for funds to the next year's business plan in order to respond to an unforeseen incident and then implement the appropriate mitigating control."

*ASSESSING COSTS*

- When asked if HCO 3 uses a quantitative approach for assessing the costs of cyber incidents, the GOCD responded in the negative. While we're "firefighting" during an incident response, he stated, it's very difficult to determine the operational cost of a specific server being down or, for that matter, the value of exfiltrated IP. "When I crash my car, it's immediately obvious what the damage is," he added, "but how do we estimate the damage from a cyber incident?"

- The RMD agreed, noting that he uses both quantitative and qualitative approaches for his more strategic risk management work, especially when it comes to assessing the potential impacts of various cyber risks to HCO 3 supply chains. He advised that his quantitative assessment in this regard begins with a fundamental measure of time – for example, how long a server is down – and ends with a standardized back-solving approach to determine the cost of an associated outage of a given duration. This calculation, the RMD explained, enables him to use an ordinal scale, normalized between 1 and 5, that assigns different parameters to estimate the overall costs of an attack on production; the state of HCO 3's preparedness; and the likelihood of a risk occurring. For qualitative purposes, he concluded, he assigns different colors to the risks assessed through this approach – red, yellow, or green – so the board can compare them visually.

- A second critical infrastructure representative responded that determining cyber incident cost impacts are not as difficult as they might initially appear. She stated that that the Department of Defense (DoD), for example, as a matter of course estimates the dollar costs of downed servers and other IT equipment attacked by APTs and other intruders.[19]

*ASSESSING BENEFITS*

- A risk manager asked the RMD how he goes about demonstrating that one security control is more effective than another for purposes of addressing a particular cyber risk. The RMD explained that he has good relationships with the investment professionals in his security portfolio who not only conduct those assessments but also make the appropriate business case to the board. "We map out three to five years for where we want to be," he stated, "and incorporate as part of our reviews an analysis of the incidents we've experienced, losses we've suffered, and the likely effectiveness of existing and new technologies to mitigate them in the future."

---

[19] Advanced Persistent Threat (APT) refers to a group, such as a government, with both the capability and intent to persistently and effectively target a specific entity. Wikipedia. Advanced Persistent Threat. ONLINE. N.D. Available: http://en.wikipedia.org/wiki/Advanced_persistent_threat [21 January 2014]. The term is commonly used to refer to cyber threats, in particular that of Internet-enabled espionage using a variety of intelligence gathering techniques to access sensitive information, but applies equally to other threats such as that of traditional espionage or attack. *Id.*

- The RMD emphasized that a key part of analyzing a security control's effectiveness involves evaluating the technical maturity of the environments in which it will be deployed. A control that might work in a developed country, he explained, might be impossible to deploy in a developing one – especially if it involves new technology that needs access to modern telecommunications networks in order to function properly. While HCO 3 prioritizes deployment of security controls to locales wherever its data centers are located, the RMD concluded, it accordingly can't deploy them in all such locales.

## *MONITORING TRAFFIC FOR INDICATORS AND EVENTS*

- In view of the CryptoLocker incident, a risk manager asked whether HCO 3 has considered decrypting all the packets leaving its network – i.e., full packet capture – as a means of preventing IP theft. The RMD responded that malicious hackers typically encrypt the "most interesting" content before it goes out, and that the capability to intercept and read it before it exits the network is therefore essential. "The members of the board are very visual," he continued, "so if you can show them that spreadsheets [rather than anonymous data packets] are on their way out the door, they immediately understand that we have a compromised machine."

- A critical infrastructure representative noted that full packet inspection of data leaving a network should itself be subject to risk analysis – not only to prioritize that traffic but also to identify, hold, and assess suspect packets that trigger alerts. He asserted that information security analysts need network optics technology to make appropriate risk management decisions about both unencrypted and encrypted data in real time. The representative noted that when it comes to encrypted packets, deep packet inspection associated with DLP solutions can help.[20] Specifically, he advised that properly configured DLP can provide sufficient context about the packets – e.g., they were obtained by abnormal access to a particular database – to justify automatically pulling them for decryption and review by analysts at a later date.

- The GOCD replied that while proactivity is a desirable goal for cyber risk management, the cost for monitoring all network traffic across the HCO 3 enterprise would be very high. He added that employees likely would not welcome the news that their personal use of network resources (e.g., online banking) is being inspected as part of a new corporate security initiative. Finally, he concluded, the Safe Harbor Privacy Principles are a significant consideration for companies like HCO 3 with an international presence and would raise significant hurdles to adopting a full packet inspection approach.[21]

---

[20] *See* DLP definition, *supra* note 8. One DLP category – advanced security measures – employs machine learning and temporal reasoning algorithms for detecting abnormal access to data and abnormal email exchange, honeypots for detecting authorized personnel with malicious intentions, and activity-based verification (e.g., recognition of keystrokes dynamics) for detecting abnormal access to data. *Id.*

[21] The Safe Harbor Privacy Principles, also known as the International Safe Harbor Privacy Principles or U.S. – EU Safe Harbor, provide a streamlined process for U.S. companies to comply with EU Directive 95/46/EC on

37

- An IT professional observed that HCO 3 is heavily involved in developing markets – including Brazil, Russia, India, and China, the so-called "BRIC" countries – where APTs are "imminently present." She then asked why, under the circumstances, HCO 3 is so focused on reactive security rather than proactive security measures. The GOCD responded that HCO 3 has taken the position that it has an Internet presence, it must assume that it's already been compromised by APTs (among others). Accordingly, while HCO 3 has made considerable investments in prevention technologies, especially perimeter defense technologies, it also must invest significantly in response – i.e., "reactive" activities. The RMD agreed, noting that a recent study had found that some 70% of companies have experienced a material cyber breach that they've chosen not to report. Given the fact that APTs are likely inside the networks of all those companies, he asserted, the primary question for them and HCO 3 is necessarily a reactive one: how fast can we find them and kick them out?

*CYBERSECURITY INSURANCE*

- A critical infrastructure representative asked how cost and benefit considerations inform HCO 3's cyber risk management decisions, including the purchase of cybersecurity insurance. The GOCD replied that HCO 3 does not currently carry cybersecurity insurance, relying instead on its aforementioned cyber risk management cycle and cyber incident run book to direct actions based on perceived costs and benefits to the company. He added that while HCO 3 is concerned about cyber risks that pose financial and/or reputational harm, both the cyber risk management cycle and cyber incident run book focus on cyber risks that could cause significant operational disruption. "The operational impact of an anticipated cyber incident determines its priority," he explained, "and directly informs the communication of an actual incident to the board."

- An IT professional then asked, given HCO 3's decision not to purchase cybersecurity insurance, whether or not HCO 3 self-insures or alternatively assumes the cost of a cyber incident when it occurs. The RMD responded that HCO 3 is actively considering whether to purchase a policy but

---

the protection of personal data. Wikipedia. International Safe Harbor Privacy Principles. ONLINE. N.D. Available: http://en.wikipedia.org/wiki/International_Safe_Harbor_Privacy_Principles [22 January 2014]. Intended for organizations within the U.S. or EU that store customer data, the Safe Harbor Privacy Principles are designed to prevent accidental information disclosure or loss. *Id*. U.S. companies can opt into the program as long as they adhere to the seven principles outlined in the directive. *Id*. They include: (1) notice – individuals must be informed that their data is being collected and about how it will be used; (2) choice – individuals must have the ability to opt out of the collection and forward transfer of the data to third parties; (3) onward transfer – transfers of data to third parties may only occur to other organizations that follow adequate data protection principles; (4) security – reasonable efforts must be made to prevent loss of collected information; (5) data integrity – data must be relevant and reliable for the purpose it was collected for; (6) access – individuals must be able to access information held about them, and correct or delete it if it is inaccurate; and (7) enforcement – there must be effective means of enforcing these rules. *Id*. The process was developed by the U.S. Department of Commerce in consultation with the EU. *Id*.

is "not yet sold" on obtaining one given the overall effectiveness of its cyber risk management cycle and its "road-mapped" cyber risk mitigations and controls. HCO 3 has only finite resources, he explained, and the debate really is whether it gets more cybersecurity bang for the buck from purchasing a policy or installing intrusion detection and other solutions that HCO 3 has pre-selected to address anticipated cyber incidents. He added that HCO 3's CISO and the company's finance office will collectively make this call.

- The RMD emphasized that HCO 3 does not question the importance of managing cyber risk – including through risk transfer to insurers – but currently believes it has a reasonably effective range of alternate mitigation approaches to do so. He added that because HCO 3 does not maintain customer PII, it may not be a company that really needs cybersecurity insurance. When asked how HCO 3 nevertheless would manage a privacy breach if one occurred, the RMD responded that the company has a privacy plan in place. "We're ultra-conservative in terms of recalling deficient products," he commented, "and in the event of a privacy data breach our privacy office will adopt a similar posture."

# CONCLUSION

Roundtable participants commented that the cyber risk management use cases highlighted the need for a sustained dialogue between cybersecurity professionals and insurers about how they could better partner for the benefit of the organizations they serve. Several noted that both communities are only now getting to know one another. A joint effort to bring about complementary cyber risk mitigation and cyber risk transfer strategies, they observed, would advance the cybersecurity cause considerably – not just for health care organizations but for entities in other sectors as well.

A critical infrastructure representative described the presenting organizations as large enterprises with "low-level cybersecurity budget and staffing." That common characteristic, he continued, suggests that their respective leaders, despite some openness to ERM, care more about governance and regulatory compliance than true cybersecurity. Another critical infrastructure representative responded that, unlike the presenting organizations, approximately 80 percent of hospitals don't have even basic awareness about their cyber risks let alone strategies to address them. He called this state of affairs, "a big problem for [the] industry." The representative added that no matter what their approach to cyber risk management, the presenting organizations accordingly should be considered advanced cybersecurity managers within the health care market.

A risk manager commented that whether an organization adopts an ERM or a "regulatory compliance" approach to cyber risk management, cybersecurity insurance can serve as a "risk reducer" by incentivizing it to adopt better security controls in return for more coverage at lower cost. He added that car manufacturers introduced anti-lock brakes because *insurers* demanded them – not regulators. An IT professional concurred, noting, "The goal of getting lower premiums will drive [cyber] risk management investments higher . . . to that end, cybersecurity insurance can be used as a market incentive." A second risk manager agreed and asserted that regulatory compliance should be abandoned as a rationale for cyber risk management investments altogether in favor of ERM approaches. He emphasized that insurance is itself an ERM issue and that teams of experts – including CISOs and other cyber risk managers – should provide their input to the "check cutters" about what kinds of coverage to purchase, for what risk transfer purposes, and in what amounts.

An insurer acknowledged the benefits of ERM but noted that insurance also could be marketed as a way to prove regulatory compliance. If an organization has cybersecurity insurance, he noted, it must adhere to certain cybersecurity requirements, some of which may be required by law. Continued adherence to those requirements as evidenced by policy renewals therefore could signal that an organization is doing what it's supposed to be doing under the contract and – by extension – the law. An organization's chief risk officer accordingly could tell its chief financial officer that, "If we have this insurance, then we don't have to separately prove that we're complying with cybersecurity regulations." The insurer concluded that this could spare organizations considerable expense. An IT professional noted that insurance likewise could be used as an attestation method to obtain incentives such as priority in government procurement.

A second insurer cautioned, however, that cybersecurity insurance should not be considered an incentive that will somehow encourage critical infrastructure owners to use the Cybersecurity Framework called for in Executive Order 13636. Instead, she asserted, carriers will assess over the next several years what positive impact that framework has on the cyber loss experiences of the organizations that use it. She observed that, based on those experiences, carriers might incorporate into their policies those framework elements that demonstrably result in better cybersecurity outcomes. The framework accordingly might have an incentivizing *effect* through insurance contracts that require an insured to incorporate proven aspects of it into their cyber risk management programs in return for new and/or more extensive coverage – i.e., for cyber-related critical infrastructure loss. Several participants responded that insurers should identify what policy, programmatic, and other initiatives should be undertaken to encourage their entry into the first-party market for this purpose.

Roundtable leaders and organizers agreed to share this feedback with DHS and NPPD senior leadership and to communicate with participants about next steps.

**Cybersecurity Insurance Roundtable**
*Health Care and Cyber Risk Management: Cost/Benefit Approaches*

**Wednesday, November 20, 2013**
**National Intellectual Property Rights Coordination Center**
2451 Crystal Drive – Suite 200
Arlington, VA 20598-5105

## AGENDA

| | |
|---|---|
| 8:00 – 8:30 | Arrival/Registration |
| 8:30 – 8:45 | Opening Remarks from DHS/NPPD |

         o    *Tom Finan, Senior Cybersecurity Strategist and Counsel*

| | |
|---|---|
| 8:45 – 9:30 | Health Care Use Case I Presentation |
| 9:30 – 10:15 | Group Discussion |
| 10:15 – 10:30 | Break |
| 10:30 – 11:15 | Health Care Use Case II Presentation |
| 11:15 – 12:00 | Group Discussion |
| 12:00 – 1:00 | Lunch (On Your Own) |
| 1:00 – 1:45 | Health Care Use Case III Presentation |
| 1:45 – 2:30 | Group Discussion |
| 2:30 – 2:45 | Break |
| 2:45 – 3:30 | Health Care Use Case IV Presentation |
| 3:30 – 4:15 | Group Discussion |
| 4:15 – 4:30 | Summary Discussion/Q&A/Close |

# Asset Management and Software Security Solutions

Tivoli Software is a brand within IBM's Cloud & Smarter Infrastructure division. Prior to being acquired by IBM in 1996, Tivoli Systems, Inc. was as an independent software vendor which developed and sold "systems management" software and services. Since the acquisition, the software portfolio has grown through development and acquisition. According to IT analyst research firm Gartner, Inc., IBM currently owns the largest share of the "IT Operations Management" software market, with an 18% market share. IBM is also the leading provider of Enterprise Asset Management software, for the 7th consecutive year, according to ARC Advisory Group, a leading research analyst firm for industry and infrastructure. Service management segments for which IBM offers software and services include the following: Cloud Management Virtualization Management Storage Management IT Service Management Application Performance Management Network Management System and Workload Automation Server, Desktop, Mobile Device Management & Security Enterprise Asset Management Facilities Management

# back office

A back office is a part of most corporations where tasks dedicated to running the company itself take place. The term "back office" comes from the building layout of early companies where the front office would contain the sales and other customer-facing staff and the back office would be those manufacturing or developing the products or involved in administration but without being seen by customers. Although the operations of a back office are seldom prominent, they are a major contributor to a business. Back offices may be located somewhere other than company headquarters. Many are in areas and countries with cheaper rent and lower labor costs. Some office parks such as MetroTech Center provide back offices for tenants whose front offices are in more expensive neighborhoods. Back office functions can be outsourced to consultants and contractors, including ones in other countries.

# Brazil

Brazil /brə z l/ (Portuguese: Brasil, IPA: [b a ziw]), officially the Federative Republic of Brazil (Portuguese: República Federativa do Brasil, listen ), is the largest country in both South America and the Latin American region. It is the world's fifth largest country, both by geographical area and by population. It is the largest Portuguese-speaking country in the world, and the only one in the Americas. Bounded by the Atlantic Ocean on the east, Brazil has a coastline of 7,491 km (4,655 mi). It borders all other South American countries except Ecuador and Chile and occupies 47.3 percent of the continent of South America. Its Amazon River basin includes a vast tropical forest and is the scene of debates over deforestation. Brazil was inhabited by numerous tribal nations prior to the landing of explorer Pedro Álvares Cabral in 1500, who claimed the area for Portugal. Brazil remained a Portuguese colony until 1808, when the capital of the empire was transferred from Lisbon to Rio de Janeiro after French forces invaded Portugal. In 1815, it was elevated to the rank of kingdom upon the formation of the United Kingdom of Portugal, Brazil and the Algarves. Its independence was achieved in 1822 with the creation of the Empire of Brazil, a unitary state governed under a constitutional monarchy and a parliamentary system. The country became a presidential republic in 1889, when a military coup d'état proclaimed the Republic, although the bicameral legislature, now called Congress, dates back to the ratification of the first constitution in 1824. An authoritarian military junta had led the nation from 1964 until 1985. Brazil's current Constitution, formulated in 1988, defines it as a federal republic. The Federation is composed of the union of the Federal District, the 26 states, and the 5,564 municipalities. The Brazilian economy is the world's seventh largest by nominal GDP and the seventh largest by purchasing power parity, as of 2012. A member of the BRIC group, Brazil until 2010 had one of the world's fastest growing major economies, with its economic reforms giving the country new international recognition and influence. Brazil's national development bank (BNDES) plays an important role for the country's economic growth. Brazil is a founding member of the United Nations, the G20, CPLP, Latin Union, the Organization of Ibero-American States, the Organization of American States, Mercosul and the Union of South American Nations. Brazil is one of 17 megadiverse countries, home to a variety of wildlife, natural environments, and extensive natural resources in a variety of protected habitats. Brazil is a regional power in Latin America and a middle power in international affairs, with some analysts identifying it as an emerging global power. Brazil has been the world's largest producer of coffee for the last 150 years. ˆ "Demographics". Brazilian Government. Archived from the original on 17 November 2011. Retrieved 8 October 2011. ˆ "Caracteristicas da População e dos Domicílios do Censo Demográfico 2010 — Cor ou raça" (PDF). Retrieved 7 April 2012. ˆ "Population Clock". ˆ ˆ Country Comparison to the World: Gini Index – Brazil The World Factbook. Retrieved on 3 April 2012. ˆ "2014 Human Development Report Summary". United Nations Development Programme. 2014. pp. 21–25. Retrieved 27 July 2014. ˆ The European Portuguese pronunciation is IPA: [b  zi ] ˆ José María Bello (1966). A History of Modern Brazil: 1889-1964. Stanford University Press. p. 56. ISBN 978-0-8047-0238-6. ˆ S. George Philander (2012). Encyclopedia of Global Warming and Climate Change, Second Edition. Princeton University. p. 148. ISBN 978-1-4129-9261-9. ˆ John J. Crocitti; Monique Vallance (2011). Brazil Today: An Encyclopedia of Life in the Republic. South Dakota State University. p. 23. ISBN 978-0-313-34673-6. ˆ a b "Geography of Brazil". The World Factbook. Central Intelligence Agency. 2008. Retrieved 3 June 2008. ˆ "BRAZIL - Land".

ˆ "Brazilian Federal Constitution" (in Portuguese). Presidency of the Republic. 1988. Retrieved 3 June 2008. "Brazilian Federal Constitution". v-brazil.com. 2007. Retrieved 3 June 2008 Unofficial translate ˆ "World Development Indicators database" (PDF file), World Bank, 7 October 2009. ˆ "CIA – The World Factbook – Country Comparisons – GDP (purchasing power parity)". Cia.gov. Retrieved 25 January 2011. ˆ Clendenning, Alan (17 April 2008). "Booming Brazil could be world power soon". USA Today – The Associated Press. p. 2. Retrieved 12 December 2008. ˆ Fernando J. Cardim de Carvalho (January 2013). "Relative insulation". D+C Development and Cooperation/ dandc.eu. ˆ "Países Membros" (in Portuguese). United Nations Information Centre Rio de Janeiro. Archived from the original on 29 March 2012. Retrieved 10 April 2013. ˆ Clare Ribando Seelke (2010). Brazil-U. S. Relations. Congressional Research Service. p. 1. ISBN 973-1-4379-2786-3. ˆ Jorge Dominguez; Byung Kook Kim (2013). Between Compliance and Conflict: East Asia Latin America and the New Pax Americana. Center for International Affairs, Harvard University. pp. 98–99. ISBN 978-1-136-76983-2. ˆ

# BRIC

In economics, BRIC is a grouping acronym that refers to the countries of Brazil, Russia, India and China, which are all deemed to be at a similar stage of newly advanced economic development. It is typically rendered as "the BRICs" or "the BRIC countries" or "the BRIC economies" or alternatively as the "Big Four". A related acronym is BRICS which includes South Africa. The acronym was coined by Jim O'Neill in a 2001 Goldman Sachs paper entitled "Building Better Global Economic BRICs." The acronym has come into widespread use as a symbol of the apparent shift in global economic power away from the developed G7 economies towards the developing world. Projections on the future power of the BRIC economies vary widely. Some sources suggest that they might overtake the G7 economies by 2027. More modestly, Goldman Sachs has argued that, although the four BRIC countries are developing rapidly, it was only by 2050 that their combined economies could eclipse the combined economies of the current richest countries of the world. In 2010, however, while the four BRIC countries accounted for over a quarter of the world's land area and more than 40% of the world's population, they accounted for only one-quarter of the world gross national income. According to a paper published in 2005, Mexico and South Korea were the only other countries comparable to the BRICs, but their economies were excluded initially because they were considered already more developed, as they were already members of the OECD. The same creator of the term "BRIC" endorsed the term MINT, that includes Mexico, Indonesia, Nigeria and Turkey. Goldman Sachs did not argue that the BRICs would organize themselves into an economic bloc, or a formal trading association, as the European Union has done. However, there are some indications that the "four BRIC countries have been seeking to form a 'political club' or 'alliance'", and thereby converting "their growing economic power into greater geopolitical clout". On June 16, 2009, the leaders of the BRIC countries held their first summit in Yekaterinburg, and issued a declaration calling for the establishment of an equitable, democratic and multipolar world order. Since then they have met in Brasília in 2010, met in Sanya, on China's Hainan Island in 2011 and in New Delhi, India, in 2012. Some other developing countries that have not yet reached the N-11 economic level, such as South Africa, aspired to BRIC status. South Africa was subsequently successful in joining the bloc, despite the fact that economists at the Reuters 2011 Investment Outlook Summit dismissed the prospects of South African success. Jim O'Neill, for example, told the summit that South Africa, at a population of under 50 million people, was just too small an economy to join the BRIC ranks. However, after the BRIC countries formed a political organization among themselves, they later expanded to include South Africa, becoming the BRICS. Several of the more developed of the N-11 countries, in particular Turkey, Mexico, Indonesia and South Korea, were seen as the most likely contenders to the BRICs. In recent years, the BRICs have received increasing scholarly attention. Brazilian political economist Marcos Prado Troyjo and French investment banker Christian Déséglise founded the BRICLab at Columbia University, a Forum examining the strategic, political and economic consequences of the rise of BRIC countries, especially by analyzing their projects for power, prosperity and prestige through graduate courses, special sessions with guest speakers, Executive Education programs, and annual conferences for policymakers, business and academic leaders, and students.

## business process

A business process or business method is a collection of related, structured activities or tasks that produce a specific service or product (serve a particular goal) for a particular customer or customers. It can often be visualized with a flowchart as a sequence of activities with interleaving decision points or with a Process Matrix as a sequence of activities with relevance rules based on data in the process.

## car manufacturers

For other automobile manufacturing related lists see See also This is a list of automobile manufacturers.

# CEO

A chief executive officer (CEO) is generally the most senior corporate officer (executive) or administrator in charge of managing a for-profit organization. The CEO of a corporation or company typically reports to the board of directors and is charged with maximizing the value of the entity. Titles often used as synonyms for CEO include president, managing director (MD) and chief executive (CE).

# chief financial officer

The chief financial officer (CFO) or chief financial and operating officer (CFOO) is a corporate officer primarily responsible for managing the financial risks of the corporation. This officer is also responsible for financial planning and record-keeping, as well as financial reporting to higher management. In some sectors the CFO is also responsible for analysis of data. The title is equivalent to finance director, a common title in the United Kingdom. The CFO typically reports to the chief executive officer and to the board of directors, and may additionally sit on the board. The CFO supervises the finance unit and is the chief financial spokesperson for the organization. The CFO reports directly to the President/Chief Executive Officer (CEO) and directly assists the Chief Operating Officer (COO) on all strategic and tactical matters as they relate to budget management, cost benefit analysis, forecasting needs and the securing of new funding.

# Chief Information Security Officer

A Chief Information Security Officer (CISO) is the senior-level executive within an organization responsible for establishing and maintaining the enterprise vision, strategy and program to ensure information assets and technologies are adequately protected. The CISO directs staff in identifying, developing, implementing and maintaining processes across the organization to reduce information and information technology (IT) risks. They respond to incidents, establish appropriate standards and controls, manage security technologies, and direct the establishment and implementation of policies and procedures. The CISO is also usually responsible for information-related compliance. Typically, the CISO's influence reaches the whole organization. Responsibilities include: Information security and information assurance Information regulatory compliance (e.g., US PCI DSS, FISMA, GLBA, HIPAA; UK Data Protection Act 1998; Canada PIPEDA) Information risk management Cybersecurity Information technology controls for financial and other systems Information privacy Computer Emergency Response Team / Computer Security Incident Response

Team Identity and access management Security Architecture IT investigations, digital forensics, eDiscovery Disaster recovery and business continuity management Information Security Operations Center ISOC Having a CISO or the equivalent function in the organization has become a standard in business, government and non-profit sectors. Throughout the world, a growing number of organizations have a CISO. By 2009, approximately 85% of large organizations had a security executive, up from 56% in 2008, and 43% in 2006. In 2011, in a survey by PricewaterhouseCoopers for their Annual Information Security Survey, 80% of businesses had a CISO or equivalent. About one-third of these security chiefs report to a Chief Information Officer (CIO), 35% to Chief Executive Officer (CEO), and 28% to the board of directors. In corporations, the trend is for CISOs to have a strong balance of business acumen and technology knowledge. CISOs are often in high demand and compensation is comparable to other C-level positions.

# chief risk officer

The chief risk officer (CRO) or chief risk management officer (CRMO) of a corporation is the executive accountable for enabling the efficient and effective governance of significant risks, and related opportunities, to a business and its various segments. Risks are commonly categorized as strategic, reputational, operational, financial, or compliance-related. CRO's are accountable to the Executive Committee and The Board for enabling the business to balance risk and reward. In more complex organizations, they are generally responsible for coordinating the organization's Enterprise Risk Management (ERM) approach. The position became more common after the Basel Accord, the Sarbanes-Oxley Act, the Turnbull Report A main priority for the CRO is to ensure that the organisation is in full compliance with applicable regulations (chief compliance officer). They may also deal with topics regarding insurance, internal auditing, corporate investigations, fraud, and information security. CRO's typically have post-graduate education and 20+ years of business experience, with actuarial, accounting, economics, and legal backgrounds common.

# Chief Technology Officer

A chief technology officer (CTO), sometimes known as a chief technical officer, is an executive-level position in a company or other entity whose occupant is focused on scientific and technological issues within an organization.

# China

China (/ t a nə/; simplified Chinese:  ; traditional Chinese:  ; pinyin: Zhōngguó), officially the People's Republic of China (PRC), is a sovereign state located in East Asia. It is the world's most populous country, with a population of over 1.35 billion. The PRC is a single-party state governed by the Communist Party, with its seat of government in the capital city of Beijing. It exercises jurisdiction over 22 provinces, five autonomous regions, four direct-controlled municipalities (Beijing, Tianjin, Shanghai, and Chongqing), and two mostly self-governing special administrative regions (Hong Kong and Macau). The PRC also claims the territories governed by the Republic of China (ROC), a separate political entity commonly known as Taiwan today, as a part of its territory, which includes the island of Taiwan as Taiwan Province, Kinmen and Matsu as a part of Fujian Province and islands the ROC controls in the South China Sea as a part of Hainan Province, a claim which is controversial due to the complex political status of Taiwan. Covering approximately 9.6 million square kilometers, China is the world's second-largest country by land area, and either the third or fourth-largest by total area, depending on the method of measurement. China's landscape is vast and diverse, ranging from forest steppes and the Gobi and Taklamakan deserts in the arid north to subtropical forests in the wetter south. The Himalaya, Karakoram, Pamir and Tian Shan mountain ranges separate China from South and Central Asia. The Yangtze and Yellow Rivers, the third- and sixth-longest in the world, run from the Tibetan Plateau to the densely populated eastern seaboard. China's coastline along the Pacific Ocean is 14,500 kilometres (9,000 mi) long, and is bounded by the Bohai, Yellow, East and South China Seas. The history of China goes back to the ancient civilization – one of the world's earliest – that flourished in the fertile basin of the Yellow River in the North China Plain. For millennia, China's political system was based on hereditary monarchies, known as dynasties, beginning with the semi-mythological Xia of the Yellow River basin (c. 2000 BCE). Since 221 BCE, when the Qin Dynasty first conquered several states to form a Chinese empire, the country has expanded, fractured and been reformed numerous times. The Republic of China (ROC) overthrew the last dynasty in 1911, and ruled the Chinese mainland until 1949. After the defeat of the Empire of Japan in World War II, the Communist Party defeated the nationalist Kuomintang in mainland China and established the People's Republic of China in Beijing on 1 October 1949, while the Kuomintang relocated the ROC government to its present capital of Taipei. China had the largest and most complex economy in the world for most of the past two thousand years, during which it has seen cycles of prosperity and decline. Since the introduction of economic reforms in 1978, China has become one of the world's fastest-growing major economies. As of 2013, it is the world's second-largest economy by both nominal total GDP and purchasing power parity (PPP), and is also the world's largest exporter and importer of goods. China is a recognized nuclear weapons state and has the world's largest standing army, with the second-largest defence budget. The PRC has been a United Nations member since 1971, when it replaced the ROC as a permanent member of the U.N. Security Council. China is also a member of numerous formal and informal multilateral organizations, including the WTO, APEC, BRICS, the Shanghai Cooperation Organization, the BCIM and the G-20. China is a regional power within Asia and has been characterized as a potential superpower by a number of commentators. ˆ Chan, Kam Wing (2007). "Misconceptions and Complexities in the Study of China's Cities: Definitions, Statistics, and Implications". Eurasian Geography and Economics 48 (4): 383–412. doi:10.2747/1538-7216.48.4.383. Archived from the original on 15 January 2013. Retrieved 7 August 2011. p. 395 ˆ a b "Law of the People's Republic of China on the Standard Spoken and Written Chinese Language (Order of the President No.37)". Chinese Government. 31 October 2000. Retrieved 21 June 2013. For purposes of this Law, the standard spoken and written Chinese language means Putonghua (a common speech with pronunciation based on the Beijing dialect) and the standardized Chinese characters. ˆ ˆ "New man at helm: Xi Jinping elected to lead China". RT.com. 15 November 2012. Retrieved 2 January 2013. ˆ "Demographic Yearbook—Table 3: Population by sex, rate of population increase, surface area and density". UN Statistics. 2007. Retrieved 31 July 2010. ˆ "China". Encyclopædia Britannica. Retrieved 16 November 2012. ˆ ˆ "Population (Total)". The World Bank. Retrieved 14 October 2014. ˆ ˆ "Population density (people per sq. km of land area)". World Bank. Retrieved 14 October 2014. ˆ a b c d "China GDP". International Monetary Fund. International Monetary Fund. Retrieved 9 October 2014. ˆ "China's Income Inequality Surpasses U.S., Posing Risk for Xi". Bloomberg. ˆ "In China, Rich Population Growth Beats World Average". Forbes. ˆ "2014 Human Development Report Summary". United Nations Development Programme. 2014. pp. 21–25. Retrieved 27 July 2014. ˆ Walton, Greg; International Centre for Human Rights and Democratic Development (2001). "Executive Summary". China's golden shield: Corporations and the development of surveillance technology in the People's Republic of China. Rights & Democracy. p. 5. ISBN 978-2-922084-42-9.

ˆ "Chinese Civil War". Cultural-China.com. Retrieved 16 June 2013. To this day, since no armistice or peace treaty has ever been signed, there is controversy as to whether the Civil War has legally ended. ˆ "Countries of the world ordered by land area". Listofcountriesoftheworld.com. Retrieved 27 April 2010. ˆ Dahlman, Carl J; Aubert, Jean-Eric. "China and the Knowledge Economy: Seizing the 21st Century. WBI Development Studies. World Bank Publications.". Institute of Education Sciences. Retrieved 26 July 2014. ˆ http://browse.oecdbookshop.org/oecd/pdfs/product/4107091e.pdf Angus Maddison. Chinese Economic Performance in the Long Run. Development Centre Studies. Accessed 2007. p.29 ˆ White, Garry (10 February 2013). "China trade now bigger than US". Daily Telegraph (London). Retrieved 15 February 2013. ˆ ˆ Muldavin, Joshua (9 February 2006). "From Rural Transformation to Global Integration: The Environmental and Social Impacts of China's Rise to Superpower". Carnegie Endowment for International Peace.

Retrieved 17 January 2010. ˆ "A Point Of View: What kind of superpower could China be?". BBC. 19 October 2012. Retrieved 21 October 2012.

# CISO

Cisco Systems, Inc. is an American multinational corporation headquartered in San Jose, California, that designs, manufactures, and sells networking equipment. The stock was added to the Dow Jones Industrial Average on June 8, 2009, and is also included in the S&P 500 Index, the Russell 1000 Index, NASDAQ-100 Index and the Russell 1000 Growth Stock Index.

# consumerproducts

In economics, any commodity which is produced and subsequently consumed by the consumer, to satisfy its current wants or needs, is a consumer good or final good. Consumer goods are goods that are ultimately consumed rather than used in the production of another good. For example, a microwave oven or a bicycle which is sold to a consumer is a final good or consumer good, whereas the components which are sold to be used in those goods are called intermediate goods. For example, textiles or transistors which can be used to make some further goods When used in measures of national income and output, the term "final goods" only includes new goods. For instance, the GDP excludes items counted in an earlier year to prevent double counting of production based on resales of the same item second and third hand. In this context the economic definition of goods includes what are commonly known as services. Manufactured goods are goods that have been processed in any way. As such, they are the opposite of raw materials, but include intermediate goods as well as final goods.

# consumer products

In economics, any commodity which is produced and subsequently consumed by the consumer, to satisfy its current wants or needs, is a consumer good or final good. Consumer goods are goods that are ultimately consumed rather than used in the production of another good. For example, a microwave oven or a bicycle which is sold to a consumer is a final good or consumer good, whereas the components which are sold to be used in those goods are called intermediate goods. For example, textiles or transistors which can be used to make some further goods. When used in measures of national income and output, the term "final goods" only includes new goods. For instance, the GDP excludes items counted in an earlier year to prevent double counting of production based on resales of the same item second and third hand. In this context the economic definition of goods includes what are commonly known as services. Manufactured goods are goods that have been processed in any way. As such, they are the opposite of raw materials, but include intermediate goods as well as final goods.

# Coordination Center

A rescue coordination centre or RCC is a primary search and rescue facility in a country that is staffed by supervisory personnel and equipped for coordinating and controlling search and rescue operations. RCC's are responsible for a geographic area, known as a "search and rescue region of responsibility" (SRR). SRR's are designated by the International Maritime Organization (IMO) and the International Civil Aviation Organization (ICAO). RCC's are operated unilaterally by personnel of a single military service (e.g. an Air Force, or a Navy) or a single civilian service (e.g. a national Police force, or a Coast Guard).

# cost/benefit analysis

Cost–benefit analysis (CBA), sometimes called benefit–cost analysis (BCA), is a systematic approach to estimating the strengths and weaknesses of alternatives that satisfy transactions, activities or functional requirements for a business. It is a technique that is used to determine options that provide the best approach for the adoption and practice in terms of benefits in labor, time and cost savings etc. (David, Ngulube and Dube, 2013). The CBA is also defined as a systematic process for calculating and comparing benefits and costs of a project, decision or government policy (hereafter, "project"). Broadly, CBA has two purposes: To determine if it is a sound investment/decision (justification/feasibility), To provide a basis for comparing projects. It involves comparing the total expected cost of each option against the total expected benefits, to see whether the benefits outweigh the costs, and by how much. CBA is related to, but distinct from cost-effectiveness analysis. In CBA, benefits and costs are expressed in monetary terms, and are adjusted for the time value of money, so that all flows of benefits and flows of project costs over time (which tend to occur at different points in time) are expressed on a common basis in terms of their "net present value." Closely related, but slightly different, formal techniques include cost-effectiveness analysis, cost–utility analysis, risk–benefit analysis, economic impact analysis, fiscal impact analysis, and Social return on investment (SROI) analysis.

# Cyber Insurance

Cyber-insurance is an insurance product used to protect businesses and individual users from Internet-based risks, and more generally from risks relating to information technology infrastructure and activities. Risks of this nature are typically excluded from traditional commercial general liability policies. Coverage provided by cyber-insurance policies may include first-party coverage against losses such as data destruction, extortion, theft, hacking, and denial of service attacks; liability coverage indemnifying companies for losses to others caused, for example, by errors and omissions, failure to safeguard data, or defamation; and other benefits including regular security-audit, post-incident public relations and investigative expenses, and criminal reward funds.

# Cybersecurity Insurance

Cybersecurity standards are security standards which enable organizations to practice safe security techniques to stop cybersecurity attacks. These guides provide general outlines as well as specific techniques for implementing cybersecurity. For certain standards, cybersecurity certification by an accredited body can be obtained. There are many advantages to obtaining certification including the ability to get cybersecurity insurance. (The choice between writing cybersecurity as two words (cyber security) or one (cybersecurity) depends on the institution, and there have been discrepancies on older documents. However, since the U.S. Federal Executive Order (EO) 13636 on the subject was spelled "Improving Critical Infrastructure Cybersecurity", most forums and media have embraced spelling "cybersecurity" as a single word.)

# Cybersecurity Insurance Roundtable

The Financial Services Roundtable (FSR) is an American financial services lobbying and advocacy organization, located in Washington, D.C.. FSR was formerly called the Bankers Roundtable, but was renamed in 2000 to reflect the widening membership of the organization beyond bank holding companies. FSR "represents 100 of the largest integrated financial services companies which provide banking, insurance and investment products and services to American consumers." The members of FSR are the CEOs of the 100 largest financial services companies with additional C-Suite level executive representatives from each company. The current President and CEO of the Financial Services Roundtable is Tim Pawlenty, who is the former governor of Minnesota.

# DAM

A dam is a barrier that impounds water or underground streams. The reservoirs created by dams not only suppress floods but provide water for various needs to include irrigation, human consumption, industrial use, aquaculture and navigability. Hydropower is often used in conjunction with dams to generate electricity. A dam can also be used to collect water or for storage of water which can be evenly distributed between locations. Dams generally serve the primary purpose of retaining water, while other structures such as floodgates or levees (also known as dikes) are used to manage or prevent water flow into specific land regions. The word dam can be traced back to Middle English, and before that, from Middle Dutch, as seen in the names of many old cities.

## data integrity

Data integrity refers to maintaining and assuring the accuracy and consistency of data over its entire life-cycle, and is a critical aspect to the design, implementation and usage of any system which stores, processes, or retrieves data. The term data integrity is broad in scope and may have widely different meanings depending on the specific context – even under the same general umbrella of computing. This article provides only a broad overview of some of the different types and concerns of data integrity. Data integrity is the opposite of data corruption, which is a form of data loss. The overall intent of any data integrity technique is the same: ensure data is recorded exactly as intended (such as a database correctly rejecting mutually exclusive possibilities,) and upon later retrieval, ensure the data is the same as it was when it was originally recorded. In short, data integrity aims to prevent unintentional changes to information. Data integrity is not to be confused with data security, the discipline of protecting data from unauthorized parties. Any unintended changes to data as the result of a storage, retrieval or processing operation, including malicious intent, unexpected hardware failure, and human error, is failure of data integrity. If the changes are the result of unauthorized access, it may also be a failure of data security. Depending on the data involved this could manifest itself as benign as a single pixel in an image appearing a different color than was originally recorded, to the loss of vacation pictures or a business-critical database, to even catastrophic loss of human life in a life-critical system.

## deep packet inspection

Deep Packet Inspection (DPI, also called complete packet inspection and Information eXtraction or IX) is a form of computer network packet filtering that examines the data part (and possibly also the header) of a packet as it passes an inspection point, searching for protocol non-compliance, viruses, spam, intrusions, or defined criteria to decide whether the packet may pass or if it needs to be routed to a different destination, or, for the purpose of collecting statistical information. There are multiple headers for IP packets; network equipment only needs to use the first of these (the IP header) for normal operation, but use of the second header (TCP, UDP etc.) is normally considered to be shallow packet inspection (usually called Stateful Packet Inspection) despite this definition. There are multiple ways to acquire packets for deep packet inspection. Using port mirroring (sometimes called Span Port) is a very common way, as well as optical splitter. Deep Packet Inspection (and filtering) enables advanced network management, user service, and security functions as well as internet data mining, eavesdropping, and internet censorship. Although DPI technology has been used for Internet management for many years, some advocates of net neutrality fear that the technology may be used anticompetitively or to reduce the openness of the Internet. DPI is used in a wide range of applications, at the so-called "enterprise" level (corporations and larger institutions), in telecommunications service providers, and in governments.

# DHS

The U.S. Department of Homeland Security (DHS) is a cabinet department of the United States federal government, first proposed by the U.S. Commission on National Security/21st Century in January 2001 and expedited in response to the September 11 attacks. The Department of Homeland Security is charged with the primary responsibilities of protecting the United States and its territories (including protectorates) from and responding to terrorist attacks, man-made accidents, and natural disasters. The Department of Homeland Security, and not the United States Department of the Interior, is equivalent to the Interior ministries of other countries. In fiscal year 2011, DHS was allocated a budget of $98.8 billion and spent, net, $66.4 billion. Where the Department of Defense is charged with military actions abroad, the Department of Homeland Security works in the civilian sphere to protect the United States within, at, and outside its borders. Its stated goal is to prepare for, prevent, and respond to domestic emergencies, particularly terrorism. On March 1, 2003, DHS absorbed the Immigration and Naturalization Service and assumed its duties. In doing so, it divided the enforcement and services functions into two separate and new agencies: Immigration and Customs Enforcement and Citizenship and Immigration Services. The investigative divisions and intelligence gathering units of the INS and Customs Service were merged forming Homeland Security Investigations. Additionally, the border enforcement functions of the INS, including the U.S. Border Patrol, the U.S. Customs Service, and the Animal and Plant Health Inspection Service were consolidated into a new agency under DHS: U.S. Customs and Border Protection. The Federal Protective Service falls under the National Protection and Programs Directorate. With more than 200,000 em-

13

ployees, DHS is the third largest Cabinet department, after the Departments of Defense and Veterans Affairs. Homeland security policy is coordinated at the White House by the Homeland Security Council. Other agencies with significant homeland security responsibilities include the Departments of Health and Human Services, Justice, and Energy. On December 16, 2013, the U.S. Senate confirmed Jeh Johnson as the Secretary of Homeland Security. According to the Homeland Security Research Corporation, the combined financial year 2010 state and local homeland security (HLS) markets, which employ more than 2.2 million first responders, totaled $16.5 billion, whereas the DHS HLS market totaled $13 billion. According to The Washington Post, "DHS has given $31 billion in grants since 2003 to state and local governments for homeland security and to improve their ability to find and protect against terrorists, including $3.8 billion in 2010". According to Peter Andreas, a border theorist, the creation of DHS constituted the most significant government reorganization since the Cold War, and the most substantial reorganization of federal agencies since the National Security Act of 1947, which placed the different military departments under a secretary of defense and created the National Security Council and Central Intelligence Agency. DHS also constitutes the most diverse merger of federal functions and responsibilities, incorporating 22 government agencies into a single organization.

# E-Government Act of 2002

The E-Government Act of 2002 (Pub.L. 107–347, 116 Stat. 2899, 44 U.S.C. § 101, H.R. 2458/S. 803), is a United States statute enacted on December 17, 2002, with an effective date for most provisions of April 17, 2003. Its stated purpose is to improve the management and promotion of electronic government services and processes by establishing a Federal Chief Information Officer within the Office of Management and Budget, and by establishing a framework of measures that require using Internet-based information technology to improve citizen access to government information and services, and for other purposes. The statute includes within it FISMA (the Federal Information Security Management Act of 2002 as Title III, and CIPSEA (the Confidential Information Protection and Statistical Efficiency Act) as Title V.

# encryption software

Encryption software is software whose main task is encryption and decryption of data, usually in the form of files on (or sectors of) hard drives and removable media, email messages, or in the form of packets sent over computer networks.

# end user

In economics and commerce, an end user is a person that uses a particular product. A product may be purchased by several intermediaries, who are not users, between the manufacturer and the end user, or be directly purchased by the end user as a consumer. For example, the end user of a pharmaceutical product is the patient who takes it, rather than distributors, pharmacists and physicians who may purchase it in their behalf. An end user of a computer system or software is someone who uses it. In contracts in some jurisdictions, the term end user is a legal term for a non-reseller. This legal construct is used in End-User License Agreements (EULAs); the end user is the user, rather than purchaser, of the subject of the Agreement.

## Enterprise Risk Management Committee

Enterprise risk management (ERM) in business includes the methods and processes used by organizations to manage risks and seize opportunities related to the achievement of their objectives. ERM provides a framework for risk management, which typically involves identifying particular events or circumstances relevant to the organization's objectives (risks and opportunities), assessing them in terms of likelihood and magnitude of impact, determining a response strategy, and monitoring progress. By identifying and proactively addressing risks and opportunities, business enterprises protect and create value for their stakeholders, including owners, employees, customers, regulators, and society overall. (ERM)... ERM can also be described as a risk-based approach to managing an enterprise, integrating concepts of internal control, the Sarbanes–Oxley Act, and strategic planning. ERM is evolving to address the needs of various stakeholders, who want to understand the broad spectrum of risks facing complex organizations to ensure they are appropriately managed. Regulators and debt rating agencies have increased their scrutiny on the risk management processes of companies.

## ERM

Erm is a village in the Netherlands and it is part of the Coevorden municipality in Drenthe. Its altitude is 14 metres (49 feet) +NAP and its population is about 420.

# ERM Council

The European Exchange Rate Mechanism (ERM) was a system introduced by the European Community on 13 March 1979, as part of the European Monetary System (EMS), to reduce exchange rate variability and achieve monetary stability in Europe, in preparation for Economic and Monetary Union and the introduction of a single currency, the euro, which took place on 1 January 1999. After the adoption of the euro, policy changed to linking currencies of EU countries outside the eurozone to the euro (having the common currency as a central point). The goal was to improve stability of those currencies, as well as to gain an evaluation mechanism for potential eurozone members. This mechanism is known as ERM II and has superseded ERM. Currently there are just two currencies in the ERM II, the Danish krone and the Lithuanian litas.

# EU

The European Union (EU) is a politico-economic union of 28 member states that are located primarily in Europe. The EU operates through a system of supranational institutions and intergovernmental negotiated decisions by the member states. The institutions are: the European Commission, the Council of the European Union, the European Council, the Court of Justice of the European Union, the European Central Bank, the Court of Auditors, and the European Parliament. The European Parliament is elected every five years by EU citizens. The EU traces its origins from the European Coal and Steel Community (ECSC) and the European Economic Community (EEC), formed by the Inner Six countries in 1951 and 1958, respectively. In the intervening years, the community and its successors have grown in size by the accession of new member states and in power by the addition of policy areas to its remit. The Maastricht Treaty established the European Union under its current name in 1993 and introduced the European Citizenship. The latest major amendment to the constitutional basis of the EU, the Treaty of Lisbon, came into force in 2009. The EU has developed a single market through a standardised system of laws that apply in all member states. Within the Schengen Area, passport controls have been abolished. EU policies aim to ensure the free movement of people, goods, services, and capital, enact legislation in justice and home affairs, and maintain common policies on trade, agriculture, fisheries, and regional development. The monetary union was established in 1999 and came into full force in 2002. It is currently composed of 18 member states that use the euro as their legal tender. Through the Common Foreign and Security Policy, the EU has developed a role in external relations and defence. The union maintains permanent diplomatic missions throughout the world and represents itself at the United Nations, the WTO, the G8, and the G-20. With a combined population of over 500 million inhabitants, or 7.3% of the world population, the EU in 2012 generated a nominal gross domestic product (GDP) of 16.584 trillion

US dollars, constituting approximately 23% of global nominal GDP and 20% when measured in terms of purchasing power parity. If it were a country, the EU would come first in nominal GDP and second in GDP (PPP) in the world. In 2012, the EU was awarded the Nobel Peace Prize.

↑ ↑ ↑ ↑ ↑ ↑ ↑ Current Article 1 of the Treaty on European Union reads:"The Union shall be founded on the present Treaty and on the Treaty on the Functioning of the European Union. Those two Treaties shall have the same legal value. The Union shall replace and succeed the European Community". ↑ http://epp.eurostat.ec.europa.eu/tgm/table.do?tab=table&language=en&pcode=tps00001&tableSelection=1 ↑ ↑ ↑ ↑ Calculated using UNDP data for the member states with weighted population. ↑ "Basic information on the European Union". European Union. europa.eu. Retrieved 4 October 2012. ↑ "European". Oxford English Dictionary. Retrieved 3 October 2011. 5 b. spec. Designating a developing series of economic and political unions between certain countries of Europe from 1952 onwards, as European Economic Community, European Community, European Union ↑ "European Union". Encyclopædia Britannica. Retrieved 3 July 2013. international organisation comprising 28 European countries and governing common economic, social, and security policies ... ↑ "European Union". The World Factbook. Central Intelligence Agency. Retrieved 11 October 2009. ↑ ↑ "Schengen area". Europa web portal. Retrieved 8 September 2010. ↑ European Commission. "The EU Single Market: Fewer barriers, more opportunities". Europa web portal. Retrieved 27 September 2007. "Activities of the European Union: Internal Market". Europa web portal. Retrieved 29 June 2007. ↑ "Common commercial policy". Europa Glossary. Europa web portal. Retrieved 6 September 2008. ↑ "Agriculture and Fisheries Council". The Council of the European Union. Retrieved 3 June 2013. ↑ "Regional Policy Inforegio". Europa web portal. Retrieved 3 June 2013. ↑ "First demographic estimates for 2009". 11 December 2009. Retrieved 3 February 2010. ↑ "European Union reaches 500 Million through Combination of Accessions, Migration and Natural Growth". Vienna Institute of Demography. ↑ ↑ "EU collects Nobel Peace Prize in Oslo". British Broadcasting Corporation. 10 December 2012. Retrieved 3 June 2013.

# EU Safe Harbor

US-EU Safe Harbor is a streamlined process for US companies to comply with the EU Directive 95/46/EC on the protection of personal data. Intended for organizations within the EU or US that store customer data, the Safe Harbor Principles are designed to prevent accidental information disclosure or loss. US companies can opt into the program as long as they adhere to the 7 principles and the 15 frequently asked questions and answers (FAQs) outlined in the Directive. The process was developed by the US Department of Commerce in consultation with the EU.

# Executive Committee

A committee (or "commission") is a type of small deliberative assembly that is usually intended to remain subordinate to another, larger deliberative assembly—which when organized so that action on committee requires a vote by all its entitled members, is called the "Committee of the Whole". Committees often serve several different functions: Governance: in organizations considered too large for all the members to participate in decisions affecting the organization as a whole, a committee (such as a Board of Directors or "Executive Committee") is given the power to make decisions, spend money, or take actions. Some or all such powers may be limited or effectively unlimited. For example of the later case, the Board of Directors can frequently enter into binding contracts and make decisions which once taken or made, cannot be taken back or undone under the law.

Coordination: individuals from different parts of an organization (for example, all senior vice presidents) might meet regularly to discuss developments in their areas, review projects that cut across organizational boundaries, talk about future options, etc. Where there is a large committee, it is common to have smaller committees with more specialized functions - for example, Boards of Directors of large corporations typically have an (ongoing) audit committee, finance committee, compensation committee, etc. Large academic conferences are usually organized by a co-ordinating committee drawn from the relevant professional body.

Research and recommendations: committees are often formed to do research and make recommendations on a potential or planned project or change. For example, an organization considering a major capital investment might create a temporary working committee of several people to review options and make recommendations to upper management or the Board of Directors. Such committees are typically dissolved after issuing recommendations (often in the form of a final report). Tabling: as a means of public relations by sending sensitive, inconvenient, or irrelevant matters to committees, organizations may bypass, stall, or disacknowledge matters without declaring a formal policy of inaction or indifference.

# Executive Committee and Risk Management

Bill Venter or William Peter Venter born 29 July 1934 Johannesburg, is a South African businessman, entrepreneur and industrialist. Venter has achieved significantly in the electronics, telecommunications and power electrical sectors, both in South Africa and abroad. He is chairman of Allied Electronics Corp Ltd (Altron), Bytes Technology Group (BTG) and the South African Council for Scientific and Industrial Research. He is on the Board of Directors of Bytes Technology Group (BTG), Power Technologies (Pty) Ltd (Powertech), Allied

Electronics Corp Ltd, Telemetrix Plc, UEC Multi-Media, Allied Technologies Ltd (Altech), AMIC Ltd., Nedcor Bank Ltd. and Standard Telephones and Cables SA. He is a Trustee of Pres Mandela's Children's Trust Fund

# Federal Government

A federation (from Latin: foedus, gen.: foederis, "covenant"), also known as a federal state, is a political entity characterized by a union of partially self-governing states or regions under a central (federal) government. In a federation, the self-governing status of the component states, as well as the division of power between them and the central government, are typically constitutionally entrenched and may not be altered by a unilateral decision of either party, the states or the federal political body. The governmental or constitutional structure found in a federation is known as federalism. It can be considered the opposite of another system, the unitary state. Germany with sixteen Länder is an example of a federation, whereas neighboring Austria and its Bundesländer was a unitary state with administrative divisions that became federated, and neighboring France by contrast has always been unitary. Federations may be multi-ethnic and cover a large area of territory (e.g. United States or India), although neither is necessarily the case. The initial agreements create a stability that encourages other common interests, reduces differences between the disparate territories, and gives them all even more common ground. At some time this is recognized and a movement is organized to merge more closely. At other times, especially when common cultural factors are at play such as ethnicity and language, some of the steps in this pattern are expedited and compressed. The international council for federal countries, the Forum of Federations, is based in Ottawa, Ontario, Canada. It helps share best practices among countries with federal systems of government, and currently includes nine countries as partner governments.

# federal law

Federal law is the body of law created by the federal government of a country. A federal government is formed when a group of political units, such as states or provinces join together in a federation, surrendering their individual sovereignty and many powers to the central government while retaining or reserving other limited powers. As a result, two or more levels of government exist within an established geographic territory. The body of law of the common central government is the federal law. Examples of federal governments include those of Australia, Brazil, Canada, Germany, Malaysia, Pakistan, Republic of India, Russia, the former Soviet Union and the United States.

# federal law enforcement

The federal government of the United States empowers a wide range of law enforcement agencies to maintain law and public order related to matters affecting the country as a whole.

# fraud

Fraud is a deception deliberately practiced in order to secure unfair or unlawful gain (adjectival form fraudulent; to defraud is the verb). As a legal construct, fraud is both a civil wrong (i.e., a fraud victim may sue the fraud perpetrator to avoid the fraud and/or recover monetary compensation) and a criminal wrong (i.e., a fraud perpetrator may be prosecuted and imprisoned by governmental authorities). Defrauding people or organizations of money or valuables is the usual purpose of fraud, but it sometimes instead involves obtaining benefits without actually depriving anyone of money or valuables, such as obtaining a drivers license by way of false statements made in an application for the same. A hoax is a distinct concept that involves deception without the intention of gain or of materially damaging or depriving the victim.

# GOCD

Gold is a chemical element with symbol Au (from Latin: aurum) and atomic number 79. It is a bright yellow dense, soft, malleable and ductile metal. The properties remain when exposed to air or water. Chemically, gold is a transition metal and a group 11 element. It is one of the least reactive chemical elements, and is solid under standard conditions. The metal therefore occurs often in free elemental (native) form, as nuggets or grains, in rocks, in veins and in alluvial deposits. It occurs in a solid solution series with the native element silver (as electrum) and also naturally alloyed with copper and palladium. Less commonly, it occurs in minerals as gold compounds, often with tellurium (gold tellurides). Gold's atomic number of 79 makes it one of the higher atomic number elements that occur naturally in the universe, and is traditionally thought to have been produced in supernova nucleosynthesis to seed the dust from which the Solar System formed. Because the Earth was molten when it was just formed, almost all of the gold present in the Earth sank into the planetary core. Therefore most of the gold that is present today in the Earth's crust and mantle is thought to have been delivered to Earth later, by asteroid impacts during the late heavy bombardment, about 4 billion years ago. Gold resists attacks by individual acids, but it can be dissolved by aqua regia (nitro-hydrochloric acid), so named because it dissolves gold into a soluble gold tetrachloride cation. Gold compounds also dissolve in alkaline solutions of cyanide, which have been used in mining. It dissolves in mercury, forming amalgam alloys; it is insoluble in nitric acid, which dissolves silver and base metals, a property that has long been used to confirm the presence of gold in items, giving rise to the term acid test. This metal has been a valuable and highly sought-after precious metal for coinage, jewelry, and other arts since long before the beginning of recorded history. In the past, a gold standard was often implemented as a monetary policy within and between nations, but gold coins ceased to be minted as a circulating currency in the 1930s, and the world gold standard (see article for details) was finally abandoned for a fiat currency system after 1976. The historical value of gold was rooted in its medium rarity, easy handling and minting, easy smelting, non-corrosiveness, distinct color, and non-reactivity to other elements. A total of 174,100 tonnes of gold have been mined in human history, according to GFMS as of 2012. This is roughly equivalent to 5.6 billion troy ounces or, in terms of volume, about 9020 m3, or a cube 21 m on a side. The world consumption of new gold produced is about 50% in jewelry, 40% in investments, and 10% in industry. Gold's high malleability, ductility, resistance to corrosion and most other chemical reactions, and conductivity of electricity have led to its continued use in corrosion resistant electrical connectors in all types of computerized devices (its chief industrial use). Gold is also used in infrared shielding, colored-glass production, and gold leafing. Certain gold salts are still used as anti-inflammatories in medicine.

## Grey Market

A grey market (sometimes called a parallel market, but this can also mean other things; not to be confused with a black market or a grey economy) is the trade of a commodity through distribution channels which, while legal, are unofficial, unauthorized, or unintended by the original manufacturer. The most common type of grey market is the sale of imported goods (brought by small import companies or individuals not authorized by the manufacturer) which would otherwise be more expensive in the country to which they are being imported. For example, importing and selling Apple products in countries such as South Korea where official Apple retail stores aren't present and licensed reseller markups are high. The two main types of grey markets are those of imported manufactured goods that would normally be unavailable or more expensive in a certain country and unissued securities that are not yet traded in official markets. Sometimes the term dark market is used to describe secretive, unregulated (though often technically legal) trading in commodity futures, notably crude oil in 2008. This can be considered a third type of "grey market" since it is legal, yet unregulated, and probably not intended or explicitly authorized by oil producers.

# handheld devices

A mobile device (also known as a handheld computer or simply handheld) is a small, handheld computing device, typically having a display screen with touch input and/or a miniature keyboard and weighing less than 2 pounds (0.91 kg). Samsung, Sony, HTC, LG, Motorola Mobility and Apple are just a few examples of the many manufacturers that produce these types of devices. A handheld computing device has an operating system (OS), and can run various types of application software, known as apps. Most handheld devices can also be equipped with Wi-Fi, Bluetooth, and GPS capabilities that can allow connections to the Internet and other Bluetooth-capable devices, such as an automobile or a microphone headset. A camera or media player feature for video or music files can also be typically found on these devices along with a stable battery power source such as a lithium battery. Early pocket-sized devices were joined in the late 2000s by larger but otherwise similar tablet computers. Much like in a personal digital assistant (PDA), the input and output of modern mobile devices are often combined into a touch-screen interface. Smartphones and PDAs are popular amongst those who wish to use some of the powers of a conventional computer in environments where carrying one would not be practical. Enterprise digital assistants can further extend the available functionality for the business user by offering integrated data capture devices like barcode, RFID and smart card readers. On July 23, 2013 it was reported that China accounts for 24% of the worlds connected devices (mainly tablets and smartphones).

# HCO

Hollister Co., often advertised as Hollister or HCo., is an American lifestyle brand owned by Abercrombie & Fitch Co. The concept was originally designed to attract consumers aged 14–18, at a lower price point than the parent brand through its SoCal and NorCal-inspired image and casual wear. Goods are available in-store and through the company's online store. It was ranked as the second most preferred clothing brand of US teens on a long list of actual West Coast companies in 2008 by Piper Jaffray.

# Healthcare Privacy Officer

The Health Insurance Portability and Accountability Act of 1996 (HIPAA; Pub.L. 104–191, 110 Stat. 1936, enacted August 21, 1996) was enacted by the United States Congress and signed by President Bill Clinton in 1996. It has been known as the Kennedy–Kassebaum Act or Kassebaum-Kennedy Act after two of its leading sponsors. Title I of HIPAA protects health insurance coverage for workers and their families when they change or lose their jobs. Title II of

HIPAA, known as the Administrative Simplification (AS) provisions, requires the establishment of national standards for electronic health care transactions and national identifiers for providers, health insurance plans, and employers.

# healthcare system

A health system, also sometimes referred to as health care system or healthcare system, is the organization of people, institutions, and resources that deliver health care services to meet the health needs of target populations. There is a wide variety of health systems around the world, with as many histories and organizational structures as there are nations. In some countries, health system planning is distributed among market participants. In others, there is a concerted effort among governments, trade unions, charities, religious organizations, or other co-ordinated bodies to deliver planned health care services targeted to the populations they serve. However, health care planning has been described as often evolutionary rather than revolutionary.

# Health Information Technology

Health information technology (HIT) is information technology applied to health care. It provides the umbrella framework to describe the comprehensive management of health information across computerized systems and its secure exchange between consumers, providers, government and quality entities, and insurers. Health information technology (HIT) is in general increasingly viewed as the most promising tool for improving the overall quality, safety and efficiency of the health delivery system. Broad and consistent utilization of HIT will: Improve health care quality or effectiveness; Increase health care productivity or efficiency; Prevent medical errors and increase health care accuracy and procedural correctness; Reduce health care costs; Increase administrative efficiencies and healthcare work processes; Decrease paperwork and unproductive or idle work time; Extend real-time communications of health informatics among health care professionals; and Expand access to affordable care. Risk-based regulatory framework for health IT September 4, 2013 the Health IT Policy Committee (HITPC) accepted and approved recommendations from the Food and Drug Administration Safety and Innovation Act (FDASIA) working group for a risk-based regulatory framework for health information technology. The Food and Drug Administration (FDA), the Office of the National Coordinator for Health IT (ONC), and Federal Communications Commission (FCC) kicked off the FDASIA workgroup of the HITPC to provide stakeholder input into a report on a risk-based regulatory framework that promotes safety and innovation and reduces regulatory duplication, consistent with section 618 of FDASIA. This provision permitted the Secretary of Health and Human Services (HHS) to form a workgroup in order to obtain broad stakeholder input from across the health care, IT, patients and innovation spectrum. The FDA, ONC, and FCC actively participated in these discussions with stakeholders from across the health care, IT, patients and innovation spectrum. HIMSS Good Informatics Practices-GIP is aligned with FDA risk-based regulatory framework for health information technology. GIP development began in 2004 developing risk-based IT technical guidance. Today the GIP peer-review and published modules are an excellent tool for educating Health IT professionals Interoperable HIT will improve individual patient care, but it will also bring many public health benefits including: Early detection of infectious disease outbreaks around the country; Improved tracking of chronic disease management; and Evaluation of health care based on value enabled by the collection of de-identified price and quality information that can be compared. According to the article published by the Internal Journal of Medical Informatics,Health information sharing between patients and providers helps to improve diagnosis, promotes self care, and patients also know more information about their health. The use of electronic medical records (EMRs) is still scarce now but is increasing in Canada, American and British primary care. Healthcare information in EMRs are important sources for clinical, research, and policy questions. Health information privacy (HIP) and security has been a big concern for patients and providers. Studies in Europe evaluating electronic health information poses a threat to electronic medical records and exchange of personal information.

# Health Information Technology for Economic and Clinical

The Health Information Technology for Economic and Clinical Health Act, abbreviated HITECH Act, was enacted under Title XIII of the American Recovery and Reinvestment Act of 2009 (Pub.L. 111–5). Under the HITECH Act, the United States Department of Health and Human Services is spending $25.9 billion to promote and expand the adoption of health information technology. The Washington Post reported the inclusion of "as much as $36.5 billion in spending to create a nationwide network of electronic health records." At the time it was enacted, it was considered "the most important piece of health care legislation to be passed in the last 20 to 30 years" and the "foundation for health care reform." The former National Coordinator for Health Information Technology, Dr. Farzad Mostashari, has explained: "You need information to be able to do population health management. You can serve an individual quite well; you can deliver excellent customer service if you wait for someone to walk through the door and then you go and pull their chart. What you can't do with paper charts is ask the question, 'Who didn't walk in the door?'"

24

# Health Insurance

Health insurance is insurance against the risk of incurring medical expenses among individuals. By estimating the overall risk of health care and health system expenses, among a targeted group, an insurer can develop a routine finance structure, such as a monthly premium or payroll tax, to ensure that money is available to pay for the health care benefits specified in the insurance agreement. The benefit is administered by a central organization such as a government agency, private business, or not-for-profit entity. According to the Health Insurance Association of America, health insurance is defined as "coverage that provides for the payments of benefits as a result of sickness or injury. Includes insurance for losses from accident, medical expense, disability, or accidental death and dismemberment" (pg. 225).

# HITECH

The Health Information Technology for Economic and Clinical Health Act, abbreviated HITECH Act, was enacted under Title XIII of the American Recovery and Reinvestment Act of 2009 (Pub.L. 111–5). Under the HITECH Act, the United States Department of Health and Human Services is spending $25.9 billion to promote and expand the adoption of health information technology. The Washington Post reported the inclusion of "as much as $36.5 billion in spending to create a nationwide network of electronic health records." At the time it was enacted, it was considered "the most important piece of health care legislation to be passed in the last 20 to 30 years" and the "foundation for health care reform." The former National Coordinator for Health Information Technology, Dr. Farzad Mostashari, has explained: "You need information to be able to do population health management. You can serve an individual quite well; you can deliver excellent customer service if you wait for someone to walk through the door and then you go and pull their chart. What you can't do with paper charts is ask the question, 'Who didn't walk in the door?' "

# identity theft

Identity theft is a form of stealing someone's identity in which someone pretends to be someone else by assuming that person's identity, usually as a method to gain access to resources or obtain credit and other benefits in that person's name. The victim of identity theft (here meaning the person whose identity has been assumed by the identity thief) can suffer adverse consequences if they are held responsible for the perpetrator's actions. Identity theft occurs when someone uses another's personally identifying information, like their name, identifying number, or credit card number, without their permission, to commit fraud or other crimes. The term identity theft was coined in 1964; however, it is not literally possible to steal an identity—less ambiguous terms are identity fraud or impersonation. "Determining the link between data breaches and identity theft is challenging, primarily because identity theft victims often do not know how their personal information was obtained," and identity theft is not always detectable by the individual victims, according to a report done for the FTC. Identity fraud is often but not necessarily the consequence of identity theft. Someone can steal or misappropriate personal information without then committing identity theft using the information about every person, such as when a major data breach occurs. A US Government Accountability Office study determined that "most breaches have not resulted in detected incidents of identity theft". The report also warned that "the full extent is unknown". A later unpublished study by Carnegie Mellon University noted that "Most often, the causes of identity theft is not known," but reported that someone else concluded that "the probability of becoming a victim to identity theft as a result of a data breach is … around only 2%". More recently, an association of consumer data companies noted that one of the largest data breaches ever, accounting for over four million records, resulted in only about 1,800 instances of identity theft, according to the company whose systems were breached. An October 2010 article entitled "Cyber Crime Made Easy" explained the level to which hackers are using malicious software. As one security specialist named Gunter Ollmann said, "Interested in credit card theft? There's an app for that." This statement summed up the ease with which these hackers are accessing all kinds of information online. The new program for infecting users' computers is called Zeus; and the program is so hacker friendly that even an inexperienced hacker can operate it. Although the hacking program is easy to use, that fact does not diminish the devastating effects that Zeus (or other software like Zeus) can do to a computer and the user. For example, the article stated that programs like Zeus can steal credit card information, important documents, and even documents necessary for homeland security. If the hacker were to gain this information, it would mean identity theft or even a possible terrorist attack.

# information technology

Information technology (IT) is the application of computers and telecommunications equipment to store, retrieve, transmit and manipulate data, often in the context of a business or other enterprise. The term is commonly used as a synonym for computers and computer networks, but it also encompasses other information distribution technologies such as television and telephones. Several industries are associated with information technology, including computer hardware, software, electronics, semiconductors, internet, telecom equipment, e-commerce and computer services. Humans have been storing, retrieving, manipulating and communicating information since the Sumerians in Mesopotamia developed writing in about 3000 BC, but the term information technology in its modern sense first appeared in a 1958 article published in the Harvard Business Review; authors Harold J. Leavitt and Thomas L. Whisler commented that "the new technology does not yet have a single established name. We shall call it information technology (IT)." Their definition consists of three categories: techniques for processing, the application of statistical and mathematical methods to decision-making, and the simulation of higher-order thinking through computer programs. Based on the storage and processing technologies employed, it is possible to distinguish four distinct phases of IT development: pre-mechanical (3000 BC – 1450 AD), mechanical (1450–1840), electromechanical (1840–1940) and electronic (1940–present). This article focuses on the most recent period (electronic), which began in about 1940.

## insurance carriers

Insurance is the equitable transfer of the risk of a loss, from one entity to another in exchange for payment. It is a form of risk management primarily used to hedge against the risk of a contingent, uncertain loss. An insurer, or insurance carrier, is a company selling the insurance; the insured, or policyholder, is the person or entity buying the insurance policy. The amount of money to be charged for a certain amount of insurance coverage is called the premium. Risk management, the practice of appraising and controlling risk, has evolved as a discrete field of study and practice. The transaction involves the insured assuming a guaranteed and known relatively small loss in the form of payment to the insurer in exchange for the insurer's promise to compensate (indemnify) the insured in the case of a financial (personal) loss. The insured receives a contract, called the insurance policy, which details the conditions and circumstances under which the insured will be financially compensated.

## insurance policies

In insurance, the insurance policy is a contract (generally a standard form contract) between the insurer and the insured, known as the policyholder, which determines the claims which the insurer is legally required to pay. In exchange for an initial payment, known as the premium, the insurer promises to pay for loss caused by perils covered under the policy language. Insurance contracts are designed to meet specific needs and thus have many features not found in many other types of contracts. Since insurance policies are standard forms, they feature boilerplate language which is similar across a wide variety of different types of insurance policies. The insurance policy is generally an integrated contract, meaning that it includes all forms associated with the agreement between the insured and insurer. In some cases, however, supplementary writings such as letters sent after the final agreement can make the insurance policy a non-integrated contract. One insurance textbook states that generally "courts consider all prior negotiations or agreements ... every contractual term in the policy at the time of delivery, as well as those written afterwards as policy riders and endorsements ... with both parties' consent, are part of written policy". The textbook also states that the policy must refer to all papers which are part of the policy. Oral agreements are subject to the parol evidence rule, and may not be considered part of the policy if the contract appears to be whole. Advertising materials and circulars are typically not part of a policy. Oral contracts pending the issuance of a written policy can occur.

## insurance policy

In insurance, the insurance policy is a contract (generally a standard form contract) between the insurer and the insured, known as the policyholder, which determines the claims which the insurer is legally required to pay. In exchange for an initial payment, known as the premium, the insurer promises to pay for loss caused by perils covered under the policy language. Insurance contracts are designed to meet specific needs and thus have many features not found in many other types of contracts. Since insurance policies are standard forms, they feature boilerplate language which is similar across a wide variety of different types of insurance policies. The insurance policy is generally an integrated contract, meaning that it includes all forms associated with the agreement between the insured and insurer. In some cases, however, supplementary writings such as letters sent after the final agreement can make the insurance policy a non-integrated contract. One insurance textbook states that generally "courts consider all prior negotiations or agreements ... every contractual term in the policy at the time of delivery, as well as those written afterwards as policy riders and endorsements ... with both parties' consent, are part of written policy". The textbook also states that the policy must refer to all papers which are part of the policy. Oral agreements are subject to the parol evidence rule, and may not be considered part of the policy if the contract appears to be whole. Advertising materials and circulars are typically not part of a policy. Oral contracts pending the issuance of a written policy can occur.

## International Safe Harbor Privacy Principles

US-EU Safe Harbor is a streamlined process for US companies to comply with the EU Directive 95/46/EC on the protection of personal data. Intended for organizations within the EU or US that store customer data, the Safe Harbor Principles are designed to prevent accidental information disclosure or loss. US companies can opt into the program as long as they adhere to the 7 principles and the 15 frequently asked questions and answers (FAQs) outlined in the Directive. The process was developed by the US Department of Commerce in consultation with the EU.

# IP addresses

An Internet Protocol address (IP address) is a numerical label assigned to each device (e.g., computer, printer) participating in a computer network that uses the Internet Protocol for communication. An IP address serves two principal functions: host or network interface identification and location addressing. Its role has been characterized as follows: "A name indicates what we seek. An address indicates where it is. A route indicates how to get there." The designers of the Internet Protocol defined an IP address as a 32-bit number and this system, known as Internet Protocol Version 4 (IPv4), is still in use today. However, due to the enormous growth of the Internet and the predicted depletion of available addresses, a new version of IP (IPv6), using 128 bits for the address, was developed in 1995. IPv6 was standardized as RFC 2460 in 1998, and its deployment has been ongoing since the mid-2000s. IP addresses are binary numbers, but they are usually stored in text files and displayed in human-readable notations, such as 172.16.254.1 (for IPv4), and 2001:db8:0:1234:0:567:8:1 (for IPv6). The Internet Assigned Numbers Authority (IANA) manages the IP address space allocations globally and delegates five regional Internet registries (RIRs) to allocate IP address blocks to local Internet registries (Internet service providers) and other entities.

# law enforcement

Law enforcement broadly refers to any system by which some members of society act in an organized manner to enforce the law by discovering, deterring, rehabilitating or punishing persons who violate the rules and norms governing that society. Although the term may encompass entities such as courts and prisons, it is most frequently applied to those who directly engage in patrols or surveillance to dissuade and discover criminal activity, and those who investigate crimes and apprehend offenders. Furthermore, although law enforcement may be most concerned with the prevention and punishment of crimes, organizations exist to discourage a wide variety of non-criminal violations of rules and norms, effected through the imposition of less severe consequences.

# malicious code

Malware, short for malicious software, is any software used to disrupt computer operation, gather sensitive information, or gain access to private computer systems. Malware is defined by its malicious intent, acting against the requirements of the computer user, and does not include software that causes unintentional harm due to some deficiency. The term badware is sometimes used, and applied to both true (malicious) malware and unintentionally harmful software. Malware may be stealthy, intended to steal information or spy on computer users for an extended period without their knowledge, as for example Regin, or it may be designed to cause harm, often as sabotage (e.g., Stuxnet), or to extort payment (CryptoLocker). 'Malware' is an umbrella term used to refer to a variety of forms of hostile or intrusive software, including computer viruses, worms, trojan horses, ransomware, spyware, adware, scareware, and other malicious programs. It can take the form of executable code, scripts, active content, and other software. Malware is often disguised as, or embedded in, non-malicious files. As of 2011 the majority of active malware threats were worms or trojans rather than viruses. In law, malware is sometimes known as a computer contaminant, as in the legal codes of several U.S. states. Spyware or other malware is sometimes found embedded in programs supplied officially by companies, e.g., downloadable from websites, that appear useful or attractive, but may have, for example, additional hidden tracking functionality that gathers marketing statistics. An example of such software, which was described as illegitimate, is the Sony rootkit, a Trojan embedded into CDs sold by Sony, which silently installed and concealed itself on purchasers' computers with the intention of preventing illicit copying; it also reported on users' listening habits, and unintentionally created vulnerabilities that were exploited by unrelated malware. Software such as anti-virus, anti-malware, and firewalls are used to protect against activity identified as malicious, and to recover from attacks.

## Management Committee

Delhi Sikh Gurdwara Management Committee or DSGMC is an autonomous organization which manages Gurudwaras in Delhi state. DSGMC also manages various educational institutions, hospitals, old age homes, libraries and other charitable institutions in Delhi. It is headquartered in Gurdwara Rakab Ganj Sahib, near Parliament House.

## National Intellectual Property Rights

The National Intellectual Property Rights Coordination Center (NIPRCC) is a U.S. government center overseen by U.S. Immigration and Customs Enforcement, a component of the U.S. Department of Homeland Security. The NIPRCC coordinates the U.S. government's enforcement of intellectual property laws. The NIPRCC was created in 2000, under the then-U.S. Customs Service as part of the implementation of the Clinton Administration's 1998 International Crime Control Strategy. The International Crime Control Strategy was developed to address the national security threat of international crime as determined by Presidential Decision Directive (PDD) 42 in 1995. The NIPRCC hosts representatives from multiple government agencies that run in the center's activities. In alphabetical order, these entities include: U.S. Customs and Border Protection Defense Criminal Investigative Service United States Department of Commerce (DOC) U.S. International Trade Administration Federal Bureau of Investigation U.S. Food and Drug Administration's Office of Criminal Investigations U.S. General Services Administration's Office of Inspector General U.S. Immigration and Customs Enforcement INTERPOL Naval Criminal Investigative Service U.S. Patent and Trademark Office U.S. Postal Inspection Service U.S. Department of State's Office of International Intellectual Property Enforcement Pilot programs are in place where representatives of the Royal Canadian Mounted Police and the Government of Mexico Tax Administration Service serve in the center in order to coordinate U.S. enforcement efforts with that of Canada and Mexico.

# National Intellectual Property Rights Coordination Center

The National Intellectual Property Rights Coordination Center (NIPRCC) is a U.S. government center overseen by U.S. Immigration and Customs Enforcement, a component of the U.S. Department of Homeland Security. The NIPRCC coordinates the U.S. government's enforcement of intellectual property laws. The NIPRCC was created in 2000, under the then-U.S. Customs Service as part of the implementation of the Clinton Administration's 1998 International Crime Control Strategy. The International Crime Control Strategy was developed to address the national security threat of international crime as determined by Presidential Decision Directive (PDD) 42 in 1995. The NIPRCC hosts representatives from multiple government agencies that run in the center's activities. In alphabetical order, these entities include: U.S. Customs and Border Protection Defense Criminal Investigative Service United States Department of Commerce (DOC) U.S. International Trade Administration Federal Bureau of Investigation U.S. Food and Drug Administration's Office of Criminal Investigations U.S. General Services Administration's Office of Inspector General U.S. Immigration and Customs Enforcement INTERPOL Naval Criminal Investigative Service U.S. Patent and Trademark Office U.S. Postal Inspection Service U.S. Department of State's Office of International Intellectual Property Enforcement Pilot programs are in place where representatives of the Royal Canadian Mounted Police and the Government of Mexico Tax Administration Service serve in the center in order to coordinate U.S. enforcement efforts with that of Canada and Mexico.

# National Protection and Programs Directorate

The National Protection and Programs Directorate (NPPD) is a component within the United States Department of Homeland Security. NPPD's goal is to advance the Department's national security mission by reducing and eliminating threats to the Nation's critical physical and cyber infrastructure. The NPPD is led by the Under Secretary of Homeland Security for National Protection and Programs, who is appointed by the President of the United States with confirmation by the United States Senate. The current Under Secretary is Suzanne E. Spaulding.

# New York Times.

The New York Times Best Seller list is widely considered the preeminent list of best-selling books in the United States. Published weekly in The New York Times Book Review, the best-seller list has been published in the Times since October 12, 1931.

# NIST 800-53

Database activity monitoring (DAM) is a database security technology for monitoring and analyzing database activity that operates independently of the database management system (DBMS) and does not rely on any form of native (DBMS-resident) auditing or native logs such as trace or transaction logs. DAM is typically performed continuously and in real-time. Database activity monitoring and prevention (DAMP) is an extension to DAM that goes beyond monitoring and alerting to also block unauthorized activities. DAM helps businesses address regulatory compliance mandates like the Payment Card Industry Data Security Standard (PCI DSS), the Health Insurance Portability and Accountability Act (HIPAA), the Sarbanes-Oxley Act (SOX), U.S. government regulations such as NIST 800-53, and EU regulations. DAM is also an important technology for protecting sensitive databases from external attacks by cybercriminals. According to the 2009 Verizon Business' Data Breach Investigations Report—based on data analyzed from Verizon Business' caseload of 90 confirmed breaches involving 285 million compromised records during 2008—75 percent of all breached records came from compromised database servers. According to Gartner, "DAM provides privileged user and application access monitoring that is independent of native database logging and audit functions. It can function as a compensating control for privileged user separation-of-duties issues by monitoring administrator activity. The technology also improves database security by detecting unusual database read and update activity from the application layer. Database event aggregation, correlation and reporting provide a database audit capability without the need to enable native database audit functions (which become resource-intensive as the level of auditing is increased)." According to a survey by the Independent Oracle User Group (IOUG), "Most organizations do not have mechanisms in place to prevent database administrators and other privileged database users from reading or tampering with sensitive information in financial, HR, or other business applications. Most are still unable to even detect such breaches or incidents." Forrester refers to this category as "database auditing and real-time protection".

## open-source software

Open-source software (OSS) is computer software with its source code made available with a license in which the copyright holder provides the rights to study, change and distribute the software to anyone and for any purpose. Open-source software is often developed in a public, collaborative manner. Open-source software is the most prominent example of open-source development and often compared to (technically defined) user-generated content or (legally defined) open-content movements. A report by the Standish Group (from 2008) states that adoption of open-source software models has resulted in savings of about $60 billion per year to consumers.

## personallyidentifiable information

"Personally identifiable information" (PII), as used in US privacy law and information security, is information that can be used on its own or with other information to identify, contact, or locate a single person, or to identify an individual in context. The abbreviation PII is widely accepted in the US context, but the phrase it abbreviates has four common variants based on personal / personally, and identifiable / identifying. Not all are equivalent, and for legal purposes the effective definitions vary depending on the jurisdiction and the purposes for which the term is being used. (In other countries with privacy protection laws derived from the OECD privacy principles, the term used is more often "personal information", which may be somewhat broader: in Australia's Privacy Act 1988 (Cth) "personal information" also includes information from which the person's identity is "reasonably ascertainable", potentially covering some information not covered by PII.) NIST Special Publication 800-122 defines PII as "any information about an individual maintained by an agency, including (1) any information that can be used to distinguish or trace an individual's identity, such as name, social security number, date and place of birth, mother's maiden name, or biometric records; and (2) any other information that is linked or linkable to an individual, such as medical, educational, financial, and employment information." So, for example, a user's IP address as used in a communication exchange is classed as PII regardless of whether it may or may not on its own be able to uniquely identify a person. Although the concept of PII is old, it has become much more important as information technology and the Internet have made it easier to collect PII through breaches of internet security, network security and web browser security, leading to a profitable market in collecting and reselling PII. PII can also be exploited by criminals to stalk or steal the identity of a person, or to aid in the planning of criminal acts. As a response to these threats, many website privacy policies specifically address the gathering of PII, and lawmakers have enacted a series of legislations to limit the distribution and accessibility of PII. However, PII is a legal concept, not a technical concept. Because of the versatility and power of modern re-identification algorithms, the absence of PII data does not mean that the remaining data does not identify individuals. While some attributes may be uniquely identifying on their own, any attribute can be identifying in combination with others.

## proactivity

In organizational behavior and industrial/organizational psychology, proactivity or proactive behavior by individuals refers to anticipatory, change-oriented and self-initiated behavior in situations, particularly in the workplace. Proactive behavior involves acting in advance of a future situation, rather than just reacting. It means taking control and making things happen rather than just adjusting to a situation or waiting for something to happen. Proactive employees generally do not need to be asked to act, nor do they require detailed instructions. Proactive behavior can be contrasted with other work-related behaviors, such as proficiency, i.e. the fulfillment of predictable requirements of one's job, or adaptability, the successful coping with and support of change initiated by others in the organization. In regard to the latter, whereas adaptability is about responding to change, proactivity is about initiating change. Proactivity is not restricted to [extra role performance] behaviors. Employees can be proactive in their prescribed role (e.g. by changing the way they perform a core task to be more efficient). Likewise, behaviors labeled as organizational citizenship behavior (OCB) can be carried out proactively or passively. For example, the altruistic OCB can be proactive in nature (e.g. offering help to co-workers before they ask for assistance).

## Programs Directorate

The National Protection and Programs Directorate (NPPD) is a component within the United States Department of Homeland Security. NPPD's goal is to advance the Department's national security mission by reducing and eliminating threats to the Nation's critical physical and cyber infrastructure. The NPPD is led by the Under Secretary of Homeland Security for National Protection and Programs, who is appointed by the President of the United States with confirmation by the United States Senate. The current Under Secretary is Suzanne E. Spaulding.

# Query Language

Query languages are computer languages used to make queries into databases and information systems. Broadly, query languages can be classified according to whether they are database query languages or information retrieval query languages. The difference is that a database query language attempts to give factual answers to factual questions, while an information retrieval query language attempts to find documents containing information that is relevant to an area of inquiry. Examples include: .QL is a proprietary object-oriented query language for querying relational databases; successor of Datalog; Contextual Query Language (CQL) a formal language for representing queries to information retrieval systems such as web indexes or bibliographic catalogues. CQLF (CODASYL Query Language, Flat) is a query language for CODASYL-type databases; Concept-Oriented Query Language (COQL) is used in the concept-oriented model (COM). It is based on a novel data modeling construct, concept, and uses such operations as projection and de-projection for multi-dimensional analysis, analytical operations and inference; DMX is a query language for Data Mining models; Datalog is a query language for deductive databases; F-logic is a declarative object-oriented language for deductive databases and knowledge representation. FQL enables you to use a SQL-style interface to query the data exposed by the Graph API. It provides advanced features not available in the Graph API. Gellish English is a language that can be used for queries in Gellish English Databases, for dialogues (requests and responses) as well as for information modeling and knowledge modeling; HTSQL is a query language that translates HTTP queries to SQL; ISBL is a query language for PRTV, one of the earliest relational database management systems; LINQ query-expressions is a way to query various data sources from .NET languages LDAP is an application protocol for querying and modifying directory services running over TCP/IP; MQL is a cheminformatics query language for a substructure search allowing beside nominal properties also numerical properties; MDX is a query language for OLAP databases; N1QL is a Couchbase's query language finding data in Couchbase Servers; OQL is Object Query Language; OCL (Object Constraint Language). Despite its name, OCL is also an object query language and an OMG standard; OPath, intended for use in querying WinFS Stores; OttoQL, intended for querying tables, XML, and databases; Poliqarp Query Language is a special query language designed to analyze annotated text. Used in the Poliqarp search engine; QUEL is a relational database access language, similar in most ways to SQL; RDQL is a RDF query language; SMARTS is the cheminformatics standard for a substructure search; SPARQL is a query language for

RDF graphs; SPL is a search language for machine-generated big data, based upon Unix Piping and SQL. SQL is a well known query language and Data Manipulation Language for relational databases; SuprTool is a proprietary query language for SuprTool, a database access program used for accessing data in Image/SQL (formerly TurboIMAGE) and Oracle databases; TMQL Topic Map Query Language is a query language for Topic Maps; Tutorial D is a query language for truly relational database management systems (TRDBMS); XQuery is a query language for XML data sources; XPath is a declarative language for navigating XML documents; XSPARQL is an integrated query language combining XQuery with SPARQL to query both XML and RDF data sources at once; YQL is an SQL-like query language created by Yahoo!

## riskmanagement

Risk management is the identification, assessment, and prioritization of risks (defined in ISO 31000 as the effect of uncertainty on objectives) followed by coordinated and economical application of resources to minimize, monitor, and control the probability and/or impact of unfortunate events or to maximize the realization of opportunities. Risks can come from uncertainty in financial markets, threats from project failures (at any phase in design, development, production, or sustainment life-cycles), legal liabilities, credit risk, accidents, natural causes and disasters as well as deliberate attack from an adversary, or events of uncertain or unpredictable root-cause. Several risk management standards have been developed including the Project Management Institute, the National Institute of Standards and Technology, actuarial societies, and ISO standards. Methods, definitions and goals vary widely according to whether the risk management method is in the context of project management, security, engineering, industrial processes, financial portfolios, actuarial assessments, or public health and safety. The strategies to manage threats (uncertainties with negative consequences) typically include transferring the threat to another party, avoiding the threat, reducing the negative effect or probability of the threat, or even accepting some or all of the potential or actual consequences of a particular threat, and the opposites for opportunities (uncertain future states with benefits). Certain aspects of many of the risk management standards have come under criticism for having no measurable improvement on risk, whether the confidence in estimates and decisions seem to increase. For example, it has been shown that one in six IT projects experience cost overruns of 200% on average, and schedule overruns of 70%.

## risk management

Risk management is the identification, assessment, and prioritization of risks (defined in ISO 31000 as the effect of uncertainty on objectives) followed by coordinated and economical application of resources to minimize, monitor, and control the probability and/or impact of unfortunate events or to maximize the realization of opportunities. Risks can come from uncertainty in financial markets, threats from project failures (at any phase in design, development, production, or sustainment life-cycles), legal liabilities, credit risk, accidents, natural causes and disasters as well as deliberate attack from an adversary, or events of uncertain or unpredictable root-cause. Several risk management standards have been developed including the Project Management Institute, the National Institute of Standards and Technology, actuarial societies, and ISO standards. Methods, definitions and goals vary widely according to whether the risk management method is in the context of project management, security, engineering, industrial processes, financial portfolios, actuarial assessments, or public health and safety. The strategies to manage threats (uncertainties with negative consequences) typically include transferring the threat to another party, avoiding the threat, reducing the negative effect or probability of the threat, or even accepting some or all of the potential or actual consequences of a particular threat, and the opposites for opportunities (uncertain future states with benefits). Certain aspects of many of the risk management standards have come under criticism for having no measurable improvement on risk, whether the confidence in estimates and decisions seem to increase. For example, it has been shown that one in six IT projects experience cost overruns of 200% on average, and schedule overruns of 70%.

## RiskManagement

Financial risk management is the practice of economic value in a firm by using financial instruments to manage exposure to risk, particularly credit risk and market risk. Other types include Foreign exchange, Shape, Volatility, Sector, Liquidity, Inflation risks, etc Similar to general risk management, financial risk management requires identifying its sources, measuring it, and plans to address them. Financial risk management can be qualitative and quantitative. As a specialization of risk management, financial risk management focuses on when and how to hedge using financial instruments to manage costly exposures to risk. In the banking sector worldwide, the Basel Accords are generally adopted by internationally active banks for tracking, reporting and exposing operational, credit and market risks.

## Risk Management

Risk management is the identification, assessment, and prioritization of risks (defined in ISO 31000 as the effect of uncertainty on objectives) followed by coordinated and economical application of resources to minimize, monitor, and control the probability and/or impact of unfortunate events or to maximize the realization of opportunities. Risks can come from uncertainty in financial markets, threats from project failures (at any phase in design, development, production, or sustainment life-cycles), legal liabilities, credit risk, accidents, natural causes and disasters as well as deliberate attack from an adversary, or events of uncertain or unpredictable root-cause. Several risk management standards have been developed including the Project Management Institute, the National Institute of Standards and Technology, actuarial societies, and ISO standards. Methods, definitions and goals vary widely according to whether the risk management method is in the context of project management, security, engineering, industrial processes, financial portfolios, actuarial assessments, or public health and safety. The strategies to manage threats (uncertainties with negative consequences) typically include transferring the threat to another party, avoiding the threat, reducing the negative effect or probability of the threat, or even accepting some or all of the potential or actual consequences of a particular threat, and the opposites for opportunities (uncertain future states with benefits). Certain aspects of many of the risk management standards have come under criticism for having no measurable improvement on risk, whether the confidence in estimates and decisions seem to increase. For example, it has been shown that one in six IT projects experience cost overruns of 200% on average, and schedule overruns of 70%.

## risk manager

Risk management is the identification, assessment, and prioritization of risks (defined in ISO 31000 as the effect of uncertainty on objectives) followed by coordinated and economical application of resources to minimize, monitor, and control the probability and/or impact of unfortunate events or to maximize the realization of opportunities. Risks can come from uncertainty in financial markets, threats from project failures (at any phase in design, development, production, or sustainment life-cycles), legal liabilities, credit risk, accidents, natural causes and disasters as well as deliberate attack from an adversary, or events of uncertain or unpredictable root-cause. Several risk management standards have been developed including the Project Management Institute, the National Institute of Standards and Technology, actuarial societies, and ISO standards. Methods, definitions and goals vary widely according to whether the risk management method is in the context of project management, security, engineering, industrial processes, financial portfolios, actuarial assessments, or public health and safety. The strategies to manage threats (uncertainties with negative consequences) typically include transferring the threat to another party, avoiding the threat, reducing the negative effect or probability of the threat, or even accepting some or all of the potential or actual consequences of a particular threat, and the opposites for opportunities (uncertain future states with benefits). Certain aspects of many of the risk management standards have come under criticism for having no measurable improvement on risk, whether the confidence in estimates and decisions seem to increase. For example, it has been shown that one in six IT projects experience cost overruns of 200% on average, and schedule overruns of 70%.

## run book

In a computer system or network, a 'runbook' is a routine compilation of procedures and operations that the system administrator or operator carries out. System administrators in IT departments and NOCs use runbooks as a reference. Runbooks can be in either electronic or in physical book form. Typically, a runbook contains procedures to begin, stop, supervise, and debug the system. It may also describe procedures for handling special requests and contingencies. An effective runbook allows other operators, with prerequisite expertise, to effectively manage and troubleshoot a system. Through runbook automation, these processes can be carried out using software tools in a predetermined manner. Runbooks are typically created by technical writers working for top tier managed service providers. They include procedures for every anticipated scenario, and generally use step-by-step decision trees to determine the effective response to a particular scenario.

## Safe Harbor Privacy Principles

US-EU Safe Harbor is a streamlined process for US companies to comply with the EU Directive 95/46/EC on the protection of personal data. Intended for organizations within the EU or US that store customer data, the Safe Harbor Principles are designed to prevent accidental information disclosure or loss. US companies can opt into the program as long as they adhere to the 7 principles and the 15 frequently asked questions and answers (FAQs) outlined in the Directive. The process was developed by the US Department of Commerce in consultation with the EU.

## SECURITY SOLUTIONS

Lockheed Martin Transportation and Security Solutions (LMTSS) is a Lockheed Martin business unit, formed of the combination of Lockheed Martin's Air Traffic Management (LMATM) unit with several other Systems Integration business units. LMTSS concentrates on Air Traffic Management and security-centric programs that involve large scale systems integration and transformational solutions. LMTSS is based in Rockville, Maryland, USA, with other major offices in Eagan, Minnesota, USA; Atlantic City, New Jersey, USA and Swanwick,

Hampshire, England and with many smaller offices in the United States and Great Britain.

## software platform

A computing platform is, in the most general sense, whatever pre-existing environment a piece of software is designed to run within, obeying its constraints, and making use of its facilities. Typical platforms include a hardware architecture, an operating system (OS), and runtime libraries. Binary executables have to be compiled for a specific hardware platform, since different central processor units have different machine codes. In addition, operating systems and runtime libraries allow re-use of code and provide abstraction layers which allow the same high-level source code to run on differently configured hardware. For example, there are many kinds of data storage device, and any individual computer can have a different configuration of storage devices; but the application is able to call a generic save or write function provided by the OS and runtime libraries, which then handle the details themselves. A platform can be seen both as a constraint on the application development process — the application is written for such-and-such a platform — and an assistance to the development process, in that they provide low-level functionality ready-made.

## software solutions

Marvell Software Solutions Israel, known as RADLAN Computer Communications Limited before 2007, is a wholly owned subsidiary of Marvell Technology Group, that specializes in local area network (LAN) technologies.

## SQL Injection

SQL injection is a code injection technique, used to attack data-driven applications, in which malicious SQL statements are inserted into an entry field for execution (e.g. to dump the database contents to the attacker). SQL injection must exploit a security vulnerability in an application's software, for example, when user input is either incorrectly filtered for string literal escape characters embedded in SQL statements or user input is not strongly typed and unexpectedly executed. SQL injection is mostly known as an attack vector for websites but can be used to attack any type of SQL database.

In a 2012 study, security company Imperva observed that the average web application received 4 attack campaigns per month, and retailers received twice as many attacks as other industries.

# supply chain management

Supply chain management (SCM) is "the systemic, strategic coordination of the traditional business functions and the tactics across these business functions within a particular company and across businesses within the supply chain, for the purposes of improving the long-term performance of the individual companies and the supply chain as a whole." It has also been defined as the "design, planning, execution, control, and monitoring of supply chain activities with the objective of creating net value, building a competitive infrastructure, leveraging worldwide logistics, synchronizing supply with demand and measuring performance globally."

# system management

Systems management refers to enterprise-wide administration of distributed systems including (and commonly in practice) computer systems. Systems management is strongly influenced by network management initiatives in telecommunications. The application performance management (APM) technologies are now a subset of Systems management. Maximum productivity can be achieved more efficiently through event correlation, system automation and predictive analysis which is now all part of APM. Centralized management has a time and effort trade-off that is related to the size of the company, the expertise of the IT staff, and the amount of technology being used: For a small business startup with ten computers, automated centralized processes may take more time to learn how to use and implement than just doing the management work manually on each computer. A very large business with thousands of similar employee computers may clearly be able to save time and money, by having IT staff learn to do systems management automation. A small branch office of a large corporation may have access to a central IT staff, with the experience to set up automated management of the systems in the branch office, without need for local staff in the branch office to do the work. Systems management may involve one or more of the following tasks: Hardware inventories. Server availability monitoring and metrics. Software inventory and installation. Anti-virus and anti-malware management. User's activities monitoring. Capacity monitoring. Security management. Storage management. Network capacity and utilization monitoring. Anti-manipulation management

# tax policy

Tax policy is the choice by a government as to what taxes to levy, in what amounts, and on whom. It has both microeconomic and macroeconomic aspects. The macroeconomic aspects concern the overall quantity of taxes to collect,

41

which can inversely affect the level of economic activity; this is one component of fiscal policy. The microeconomic aspects concern issues of fairness (who to tax) and allocative efficiency (i.e., which taxes will have how much of a distorting effect on the amounts of various types of economic activity).

## telecommunications networks

A telecommunications network is a collection of terminal nodes, links and any intermediate nodes which are connected so as to enable telecommunication between the terminals. The transmission links connect the nodes together. The nodes use circuit switching, message switching or packet switching to pass the signal through the correct links and nodes to reach the correct destination terminal. Each terminal in the network usually has a unique address so messages or connections can be routed to the correct recipients. The collection of addresses in the network is called the address space. Examples of telecommunications networks are: computer networks the Internet the telephone network the global Telex network the aeronautical ACARS network Benefits of Telecommunications and Networking Telecommunications can greatly increase and expand resources to all types of people. For example, businesses need a greater telecommunications network if they plan to expand their company. With Internet, computer, and telephone networks, businesses can allocate their resources efficiently. These core types of networks will be discussed below: Computer Network: A computer network consists of computers and devices connected to one another. Information can be transferred from one device to the next. For example, an office filled with computers can share files together on each separate device. Computer networks can range from a local network area to a wide area network. The difference between the types of networks is the size. These types of computer networks work at certain speeds, also known as broadband. The Internet network can connect computer worldwide. Internet Network: Access to the network allows users to use many resources. Over time the Internet network will replace books. This will enable users to discover information almost instantly and apply concepts to different situations. The Internet can be used for recreational, governmental, educational, and other purposes. Businesses in particular use the Internet network for research or to service customers and clients. Telephone Network: The telephone network connects people to one another. This network can be used in a variety of ways. Many businesses use the telephone network to route calls and/or service their customers. Some businesses use a telephone network on a greater scale through a private branch exchange. It is a system where a specific business focuses on routing and servicing calls for another business. Majority of the time, the telephone network is used around the world for recreational purposes.

# theft

In common usage, theft is the taking of another person's property without that person's permission or consent with the intent to deprive the rightful owner of it. The word is also used as an informal shorthand term for some crimes against property, such as burglary, embezzlement, larceny, looting, robbery, shoplifting, library theft, and fraud (i.e., obtaining money under false pretenses. In some jurisdictions, theft is considered to be synonymous with larceny; in others, theft has replaced larceny. Someone who carries out an act of or makes a career of theft is known as a thief. The act of theft is known by terms such as stealing, thieving, wicksing, and filching. Theft is the name of a statutory offence in California, Canada, England and Wales, Hong Kong, Northern Ireland, the Republic of Ireland, and Victoria.

## Times Square

Times Square is a major commercial intersection and a neighborhood in Midtown Manhattan, New York City, at the junction of Broadway (now converted into a pedestrian plaza) and Seventh Avenue and stretching from West 42nd to West 47th Streets. Brightly adorned with billboards and advertisements, Times Square is sometimes referred to as "The Crossroads of the World", "The Center of the Universe", and the heart of "The Great White Way". It is the hub of the Broadway Theater District, one of the world's busiest pedestrian intersections, and a major center of the world's entertainment industry. Times Square is one of the world's most visited tourist attractions, drawing over 39 million visitors annually. Approximately 330,000 people pass through Times Square daily, many of whom are either tourists or people working in the area. Formerly Longacre Square, Times Square was renamed in April 1904 after The New York Times moved its headquarters to the newly erected Times Building (now called One Times Square), the site of the annual ball drop on New Year's Eve, a tradition which began on December 31, 1907 and continues today, attracting thousands to the Square every New Year's Eve. The northern triangle of Times Square is Duffy Square, which was dedicated in 1937 to Chaplain Francis P. Duffy of New York City's "Fighting 69th" Infantry Regiment; a memorial to Duffy is located there, along with a statue of George M. Cohan, and the TKTS discount theatre tickets booth. The stepped red roof of the TKTS booth also provides seating for various events. The statue of Duffy and Duffy Square were listed on the National Register of Historic Places in 2001.

## Trustees Audit Committee

Victor van der Chijs (born in Ede, Netherlands, 1960) is a Dutch entrepreneur. Since October 1, 2013 he is the President of the Executive Board of the University of Twente, the highest managing body of this university. The University of Twente is a technical university that offers research and degree programmes in engineering and in the social and behavioral sciences. In keeping with its entrepreneurial spirit, the university is committed to making economic and social contribution to society. Van der Chijs is currently re-evaluating the strategic direction of the university under the flag of Vision 2020, Together with students, staff, alumni and external stakeholders of the University of Twente, he is working on a more focused strategy for the future of the university, with the aim of finding solutions for major social issues.

# U.S.

The United States of America (USA or U.S.A.), commonly referred to as the United States (US or U.S.), America, and sometimes the States, is a federal republic consisting of 50 states and a federal district. The 48 contiguous states and Washington, D.C., are in central North America between Canada and Mexico. The state of Alaska is the northwestern part of North America and the state of Hawaii is an archipelago in the mid-Pacific. The country also has five populated and nine unpopulated territories in the Pacific and the Caribbean. At 3.80 million square miles (9.85 million km2) and with around 318 million people, the United States is the world's third- or fourth-largest country by total area and third-largest by population. It is one of the world's most ethnically diverse and multicultural nations, the product of large-scale immigration from many countries. The geography and climate of the United States is also extremely diverse, and it is home to a wide variety of wildlife. Paleo-Indians migrated from Eurasia to what is now the U.S. mainland around 15,000 years ago, with European colonization beginning in the 16th century. The United States emerged from 13 British colonies located along the Atlantic seaboard. Disputes between Great Britain and these colonies led to the American Revolution. On July 4, 1776, as the colonies were fighting Great Britain in the American Revolutionary War, delegates from the 13 colonies unanimously issued the Declaration of Independence. The war ended in 1783 with the recognition of independence of the United States from the Kingdom of Great Britain, and was the first successful war of independence against a European colonial empire. The current Constitution was adopted on September 17, 1787. The first ten amendments, collectively named the Bill of Rights, were ratified in 1791 and designed to guarantee many fundamental civil rights and freedoms. Driven by the doctrine of manifest destiny, the United States embarked on a vigorous expansion across North America throughout the 19th century. This involved displacing native tribes, acquiring new territories, and gradually admitting new states. During the second half of the 19th century, the American Civil War ended legal slavery in the country. By the end of that century, the United States extended into the Pacific Ocean, and its economy began to soar. The Spanish–American War and World War I confirmed the country's status as a global military power. The United States emerged from World War II as a global superpower, the first country to develop nuclear weapons, the only country to use them in warfare, and as a permanent member of the United Nations Security Council. The end of the Cold War and the dissolution of the Soviet Union left the United States as the sole superpower. The United States is a developed country and has the world's largest national economy. The economy is fueled by an abundance of natural resources and high worker productivity. While the U.S. economy is considered post-industrial, it continues to be one of the world's largest manufacturers. The country accounts for 37% of global military spending, being the world's foremost economic and military power, a prominent political and cultural force, and a leader in scientific research and technological innovations.

# U.S. Department of Commerce

The United States Department of Commerce (DOC) is the Cabinet department of the United States government concerned with promoting economic growth. The mission of the department is to "promote job creation and improved living standards for all Americans by creating an infrastructure that promotes economic growth, technological competitiveness, and sustainable development". Among its tasks are gathering economic and demographic data for business and government decision-making, issuing patents and trademarks, and helping to set industrial standards. The Department of Commerce headquarters is the Herbert C. Hoover Building in Washington, D.C.

# Virginia

Virginia (/vər d njə/), officially the Commonwealth of Virginia, is a U.S. state located in the South Atlantic region of the United States. Virginia is nicknamed the "Old Dominion" due to its status as a former dominion of the English Crown, and "Mother of Presidents" due to the most U.S. presidents having been born there. The geography and climate of the Commonwealth are shaped by the Blue Ridge Mountains and the Chesapeake Bay, which provide habitat for much of its flora and fauna. The capital of the Commonwealth is Richmond; Virginia Beach is the most populous city, and Fairfax County is the most populous political subdivision. The Commonwealth's estimated population as of 2013 is over 8.2 million. The area's history begins with several indigenous groups, including the Powhatan. In 1607 the London Company established the Colony of Virginia as the first permanent New World English colony. Slave labor and the land acquired from displaced Native American tribes each played a significant role in the colony's early politics and plantation economy. Virginia was one of the 13 Colonies in the American Revolution and joined the Confederacy in the American Civil War, during which Richmond was made the Confederate capital and Virginia's northwestern counties seceded to form the state of West

Virginia. Although the Commonwealth was under single-party rule for nearly a century following Reconstruction, both major national parties are competitive in modern Virginia. The Virginia General Assembly is the oldest continuous law-making body in the New World. The state government has been repeatedly ranked most effective by the Pew Center on the States. It is unique in how it treats cities and counties equally, manages local roads, and prohibits its governors from serving consecutive terms. Virginia's economy has many sectors: agriculture in the Shenandoah Valley; federal agencies in Northern Virginia, including the headquarters of the Department of Defense and CIA; and military facilities in Hampton Roads, the site of the region's main seaport. Virginia's economy transitioned from primarily agricultural to industrial during the 1960s and 1970s, and in 2002 computer chips became the state's leading export.

# Wikipedia

Wikipedia (/ w k pi diə/ or / w ki pi diə/ WIK-i-PEE-dee-ə) is a free-access, free content Internet encyclopedia, supported and hosted by the non-profit Wikimedia Foundation. Anyone who can access the site can edit almost any of its articles. Wikipedia is the sixth-most popular website and constitutes the Internet's largest and most popular general reference work. Jimmy Wales and Larry Sanger launched Wikipedia on January 15, 2001. Sanger coined its name, a portmanteau of wiki (from the Hawaiian word for "quick") and encyclopedia. Although Wikipedia's content was initially only in English, it quickly became multilingual, through the launch of versions in different languages. All versions of Wikipedia are similar, but important differences exist in content and in editing practices. The English Wikipedia is now one of more than 200 Wikipedias, but remains the largest one, with over 4.6 million articles. As of February 2014, it had 18 billion page views and nearly 500 million unique visitors each month. Wikipedia has more than 22 million accounts, out of which there were over 73,000 active editors globally as of May 2014. Studies tend to show that Wikipedia's accuracy is similar to Encyclopedia Britannica, with Wikipedia being much larger. However, critics have worried that Wikipedia exhibits systemic bias, and that its group dynamics hinder its goals. Most academics, historians, teachers and journalists reject Wikipedia as a reliable source of information for being a mixture of truths, half truths, and some falsehoods, and that as a resource about controversial topics, Wikipedia is notoriously subject to manipulation and spin. Wikipedia's Consensus and Undue Weight policies have been repeatedly criticised by prominent scholarly sources for undermining freedom of thought and leading to false beliefs based on incomplete information.

# wireless network

A wireless network is any type of computer network that uses wireless data connections for connecting network nodes. Wireless networking is a method by which homes, telecommunications networks and enterprise (business) installations avoid the costly process of introducing cables into a building, or as a connection between various equipment locations. Wireless telecommunications networks are generally implemented and administered using radio communication. This implementation takes place at the physical level (layer) of the OSI model network structure. Examples of wireless networks include cell phone networks, Wi-Fi local networks and terrestrial microwave networks.